# THE 700 HABITS OF HIGHLY INEFFECTIVE PEOPLE

## AND HOW YOU CAN AVOID FALLING INTO THEM

JONATHAN BIGGINS

**WARNING: MAY NOT CONTAIN 700 HABITS**

MELBOURNE UNIVERSITY PRESS
An imprint of Melbourne University Publishing Limited
187 Grattan Street, Carlton, Victoria 3053, Australia
mup-info@unimelb.edu.au
www.mup.com.au

First published 2007
Text © Jonathan Biggins, 2007
Design and typography © Melbourne University Publishing Limited, 2007

This book is copyright. Apart from any use permitted under the *Copyright Act 1968* and subsequent amendments, no part may be reproduced, stored in a retrieval system or transmitted by any means or process whatsoever without the prior written permission of the publishers. Every attempt has been made to locate the copyright holders for material quoted in this book. Any person or organisation that may have been overlooked or misattributed may contact the publisher.

Designed by Nada Backovic Designs
Typeset by Megan Ellis
Printed in Australia by Griffin Press

National Library of Australia Cataloguing-in-Publication entry:
Biggins, Jonathan.

The 700 habits of highly ineffective people: and how you
can avoid falling into them.

ISBN 978 0 522 85365 0 (pbk.).

1. Performance standards —Humour. 2. Success in business—
Humour. I. Title. II. Title: Seven hundred habits of highly
ineffective people.

158.10207

# CONTENTS

| | | |
|---|---|---|
| Introduction | | v |
| 1 | What Is an *Effective* Person? | 1 |
| 2 | First Principles | 7 |
| 3 | The Ground's the Limit | 13 |
| 4 | The Top Ten | 25 |
| 5 | What's the Rush? | 33 |
| 6 | Fear of Disappointment | 43 |
| 7 | Communication, or Getting What You Want to Say Over in the Best Sort-of, like, Way Possible | 55 |
| 8 | It's a Worry | 73 |
| 9 | Well, If That's What You Think of Me | 85 |
| 10 | Putting It Together: Organise! | 91 |
| 11 | Let's Get Personal | 115 |
| 12 | On the Home Front | 131 |
| 13 | Special Occasions | 167 |
| 14 | The Home Handyperson | 187 |
| 15 | The Parent Crap | 201 |

| 16 Ignoring History | 217 |
|---|---|
| 17 Why Can't I Have That? | 231 |
| 18 Is That All There Is? | 241 |
| Further Reading | 247 |

# INTRODUCTION

'Only mediocrity can be trusted to be always at its best.'
*Max Beerbohm 1872–1956*

'You can do no more than do your best.'
*Anon.*

People may well ask: who is this book for? Well, one person has, and she was in marketing. To narrow it down, this is a book for almost everyone who wakes up in the morning. (It may be a bit late for anyone else but stranger things have happened.) It's a book for the try-hards and losers, the strivers and optimists, the also-rans and wannabes. For the cannon fodder, the plodders, those who are still the Indigenous Native Americans when there are too many Chiefs; the bronze medallists or the mildly disappointed bringing up the rear, the special people, the plain Janes with great personalities, the people who never seem to know when they've made their point.

Every day, we're told to improve ourselves. Lose weight, work harder, spend more time with our families, eat seven servings of vegetables a day. An industry has burgeoned to show us how to time-manage, remove unsightly cellulite or walk over hot coals to make us harder, hungrier salespersons. But unlike those self-help books, which set strategies to reach unrealistic goals like personal fulfilment, happiness or an indexed growth pension that keeps up with *real* inflationary figures, this is a book that points the way ahead by simply telling you what **not** to do. No gratuitous advice, just a few simple warning signs of the traps and pitfalls to avoid. If you do **nothing** that's listed in the following pages, you'll be a better person. Slightly. It's as simple and rewarding as that.

You're about to discover a system called **Passive Improvement**™, a lifestyle enhancement program specifically designed for those who simply cannot be bothered. For people who think pro-active is some kind of dietary fibre supplement. Life's already complicated enough. Why make it more difficult?

By examining the historical and statistical evidence, we'll demonstrate that the odds of you 'having it all' are marginally worse than those of the Maldives winning the rugby World Cup. So we'll redefine the notions of **success** and **effectiveness** and look at what it takes to lift you just off the bottom of the pile. Simply by studying at your leisure the 700 Habits of losers who are even further down the food chain than you are, you can elevate your own sense of self-worth to a higher plane. Throughout the book, you'll discover some of history's more notorious highly ineffective people and you can learn from their experiences, so if you make the mistakes they made at least you'll know you're not alone.

But remember: not everyone can be Tom Cruise—and even fewer want to be. We're all in the same lifeboat drifting on the sea of uncertainty; it's just that some of us have food, water and sunscreen. I want you to think about this simple challenge: dare to demand less.

# 1
# WHAT IS AN *EFFECTIVE* PERSON?

'There's no secret about success. Did you ever meet a successful man who didn't tell you about it?'
*Kim Hubbard*

This page has been unintentionally left blank.

The **ineffective** are defined by default, only revealed when held in stark relief against those who are considered **effective**. Modern effectiveness is primarily associated with efficiency, an ability to complete a set of evaluative tasks that can be benchmarked against a social standard. It's a legacy that goes back to the industrial revolution, when work became the defining factor in our lives and we moved from a co-operative model of existence to a competitive one. We were effectively sold the myth that work would make us free.

Ever since, our effectiveness as human beings has been largely determined by our effectiveness as producers / consumers, with occasional lip service being paid to our abilities as friends, partners, parents or concerned citizens. The arbiters of the standards by which we're all judged have shifted from the medieval dominance of a moral church to a hybrid of the media, the corporate world, our civic institutions, and governments compliant to a somewhat hazy notion of free-market social democracy.

Under the societal urge to constantly self-improve, effectiveness dangles as a carrot to tempt the effective to strive even harder; it hangs threateningly as a stick to drive the ineffective to clean up their act and get on with it.

Today's effectiveness evaluation begins in childhood, with the modern obsession for small children to reach developmental milestones at an appropriate age so they can be judged normal or otherwise. Schools are increasingly being asked to continue the process, with report cards that label each student on a sliding scale between success and failure. 'Gifted' children can then be accelerated, presumably towards the brick wall of adulthood, while those falling behind can line up future jobs in the hospitality industry. An Australian study of parental attitudes to schooling found that 80 per cent of the parents surveyed thought of their children as gifted, which says far more about *them* and the pressure of expectation than it does about their budding geniuses. Our children's effectiveness is seen as a positive reflection on our own. Bad news: to be Mozart is to be gifted; to be able to identify dinosaurs and count to ten in Esperanto at the age of four is not.

Education continues as a competitive sport, with the universities becoming glorified vocational training centres and the truly glittering prizes being offered only to those who reach the top in the subjects best suited to the market. Forget Lord Byron and the wistful gaze of poesy; the quadrangle is the culling yard where the strongest get their MBAs or law degrees and the rest get a lifetime of debt and a pointless working knowledge of existentialism.

**Habit 48       Believing in the wistful gaze of poesy**

## What Is an *Effective* Person?

Alternatively, the effective work their way up through the School of Hard Knocks, the alma mater most favoured by talkback hosts, doing the hard yards (or difficult metres in the metric system) and clawing their way up through the ranks of small business until they're running their own equipment hire franchise, or whatever—even though they left school at twelve and worked double shifts at McDonald's to pay for the rent and their parents' gambling habits. Meanwhile, the rest of us are still flipping burgers or cleaning the hire equipment out the back.

Having ascended thus far, the effective squire their dynasties and extend their sphere of influence through local sporting groups, golf clubs, schools and business associations. They effortlessly juggle a demanding schedule of extended work hours, child-rearing, holidays, self-improvement, glittering social occasions, exercise, consumerism, financial planning, private health care, share portfolios, promotion, some sort of art or craft, trophies, second cars, boats, flat-screen TVs, leisure activities and pre-arranged funerals.

In today's world, the effective are capable of multi-tasking, time management, self-fulfilment and arranging a retirement that adequately reflects their monetary aspirations for an ever-increasing lifespan. They are results-based: their efforts can be recognised, evaluated and rewarded. The same needs to be adjudged of those around them, because the effective can only succeed if their families are seen to be succeeding as well. They must be able to instigate their own advancement, be pro-active and self-interested, yet still find time to give a little to the bush fire brigade and the Cancer Council. They are patriotic, are moderate in their views and avoid indulging to excess. They believe in the competitive benefits of privatisation and in the profit motive and they usually hold some sort of religious or spiritual belief. Recognising that there is always room for improvement, they will seek to maximise their potential, through career-oriented self-education, personal coaching, fitness instruction and allocation of quality time.

In a word, **nauseating**.

# 2
# FIRST PRINCIPLES

'The man who moves a mountain begins by carrying away small stones.'
*Chinese Proverb (of the bleedin' obvious)*

This page may be recycled.

One of the ten commandments of the self-help movement is **Make a List**. And who doesn't like making a list? Well, there's always the:

- non-prioritisers
- randomalists
- linear thinkers
- dyslexics
- illiterate or innumerate
- people with an irrational fear of savants.

... but apart from them, anyone who's anyone loves a list. Let's begin with an example:

## SOME OF THE HABITS OF HIGHLY INEFFECTIVE PEOPLE

### 56 Buying self-help books

The first self-help book of the modern era was the imaginatively titled *Self Help*, written by Samuel Smiles in 1859. Espousing the virtues of hard work, thrift and temperance, it was based on the central premise of all personal improvement books: you, the reader, in some way feel inadequate but rest assured, there is a better life for you somewhere else and only I, the author, know the secret of how to take you there.

It's a secret that's made some people very rich. According to Steve Salerno, author of *SHAM—How the Gurus of the Self-Help Movement Make Us Helpless*, the self-help and actualisation movement in the United States alone was worth US$8.56 billion a year in 2005 and was expected to reach US$12 billion by 2008. Antony Robbins, the motivational guru's guru, has an estimated annual income of US$80 million, much of it derived from repeat business. It seems that once you've woken the sleeping giant within, it keeps hitting the snooze button and has to be woken up all over again.

Indeed, the fact that millions, possibly billions, of books offering variations on the one central theme have been sold since 1859 (and let's not even count the number of bibles that have changed hands) suggests that few—if any—have actually mapped the definitive path to success and it remains an elusive, flickering lighthouse beckoning to us all, cut off by a fast-approaching tide. Or perhaps success is merely an optical illusion, all the more powerful in its hold over us because it's a figment of our imaginations. There's a book in that. In fact there have been several—*The Road Less Traveled* by M Scott Peck, for one.

The value of the self-actualisation movement is best put into perspective by remembering that most of the people running the world today have bought self-help books—some have even read them. Yet how much worse does the world have to get before someone suggests heading back to the drawing board as a matter of urgency?

## 33 Having insensitive friends

This book may have been bought for you by a concerned friend. The ineffective maintain dubious friendships because often they feel lucky to have any friends at all and tend to latch onto whoever's going spare.

## 145 Not sticking to a plan

It's difficult for HIP (Highly Ineffective People) to think sequentially and move from Point A to Point B before attempting the shift to Point C. And that's assuming they've drawn up a plan in the first place. Here are the statistics:

- Unless specifically instructed to do so, 82% of people don't make a plan.
- For the 18% who do, the plan is to one day make a plan.
- Of the 15% of the 18% that move beyond the primary stage and actually make a plan...
- Only 10% stick to it.

Which means that out of a sample group of 100 people, only 0.27 of a person will persevere with a plan. So theoretically, you need at least 400 people to find one plan with any chance of success. That is why there are so few leaders, so many followers.

## 349 Making up statistics to support your argument

Guilty as charged. The above statistical data on plan-making is illustrative only but I challenge anyone to prove it's not accurate.

## 27 Repeating yourself

It's not just old people—although, statistically, old people are more ineffective than most. Chances are you've found yourself in a work situation—or an *employment environment*—silently screaming at someone who happens to be below retirement age: 'If he tells me the wisdom teeth story one more time I'm going to take them out for him!'

You've fallen victim to a Repeat Anecdote Offender. Let's look at how the RAO is ineffective. They're:

- ❖ wasting your time
- ❖ wasting their time
- ❖ wasting company time
- ❖ practising inadequate preventative dental care
- ❖ dull.

And it's not just anecdotes. HIP will always repeat instructions (because ill-conceived directives always need reiteration) and suggestions (because they've only got one).

## 22 Going like a bull at a gate

The ineffective just charge at things with no sense of order, there's no thinking ahead and what you end up with is this big kind of mess thing, where nothing's in the right place, the habits are out of order, it doesn't sense make and it just falls in a heap…

Point taken?

# 3
# THE GROUND'S THE LIMIT

'If at first you don't succeed, failure may be more your style.'
*Quentin Crisp*

This page is inserted to make the book look bigger.

The last chapter showed us just what sort of minefield the highly ineffective have to negotiate each day. Habits of ineffectiveness proliferate exponentially: one leads to ten others, the ten to a hundred and the hundred to a much bigger number. Take a quick look at the following seven habits.

**11 Aiming too high**

**12 Abreviatng**

**13 Thinking you can have it all**

**14 Believing the leader is the ladder**

**15 Reading *Playboy* magazine for the book reviews**

**16 Equating material gain with success**

**17 Not distinguishing dream from fantasy**

**704 Having poor arithmetical skills**

Okay, you probably spotted the trick one—nobody reads *Playboy* magazine for the book reviews. But if any of those habits sound familiar, it may be that you need to redefine **effectiveness** and **success**.

Let's take an example. We all know Ian Thorpe, former Australian world champion Olympic swimmer, who won heaps of gold medals and looks good in a string of pearls. He got to the top because he followed his dreams, believed in himself, dug deep and wanted it bad. To a point. But the **real** reason he made it to the top of international swimming is this: he was a very good swimmer. He was exceptionally good at going quickly from one end of a pool to the other and then repeating it. For him, the hardest part was counting the laps. He was a natural, born to it, and someone was smart enough to spot the fact and get him down to the pool every morning for ten years to swim up and down like a dolphin with an obsessive–compulsive disorder.

But would Thorpey, given the same amount of self-belief, determination and taxpayer support at the Australian Institute of Sport, have made it to the top of international chess? No, because he's crap at chess. He was smart enough to realise his **limitations** in all chess-related spheres and stuck to the swimming instead. He reached the top because he was **effective** and knew how to swim; he was **successful** because he achieved what he was **capable** of.

Are you a good swimmer? Have you been born with an unnatural ability to propel yourself through water at a faster rate than any of the six billion people on the planet who have access to a fifty metre pool? **Probably not**. So realise your limitations and set your sights accordingly.

Or maybe you have trouble distinguishing dream from fantasy. How often have you been exhorted to 'Follow your dreams'? There is a fundamental problem with following your dreams: dreams are not real. They're a series of loosely connected mental pictures that synapses in your brain create while you're asleep. Dreams are so insubstantial, you don't even wake up for them. It's the manifestations of our deep-seated fears—our nightmares—that actually rouse us to consciousness.

Think about a dream you had last night. You know, the one where you were in a strange house and the floor was made of plastic bags and your best friend was in it but it wasn't really her, it was sort of an amalgam of her and a girl who was at your school for, like, only one term but a real bitch and you've never forgotten her because she gobbed in your pencil case during history but then there was this real weird bit where she turned into a gazelle and you ate her back legs but she could still sort of walk …

Now what would be the point of following that? Have you had one dream in your life that made any kind of sense? And let's be honest here: have you ever paid attention to a single word that anyone has uttered after saying 'I had this amazing dream last night …'?

## 18  Telling other people your dreams

Worse still are the dreams that beguile the waking hours, idle fancies of future triumphs as you gaze out the window. If you can't even concentrate on the job in hand, how are you going to find a cure for cancer or be the first woman on the moon?

Okay, maybe you've dreamed of being Ian Thorpe and winning a gold medal. That's not a dream—that's a **fantasy**.

And for some people of certain persuasions I'm sure it's a pleasant fantasy, but get real: if you weigh 128 kilos and have trouble dog-paddling between the lane dividers you can dream about Ian Thorpe as much as you like; it's not going to happen. Don't **aim too high**.

## 19 Having poor spatial awareness and limited graphic skills

This may make it difficult for you to interpret the following complex diagram explaining the relationship between aspirations and the potential which is shaped by your limitations.

Aspirations ⟶

Limitations ⟶

The **aspirations** are bigger than the **limitations**. In other words, you're hoping for more than you can possibly achieve. In psychological terms, this is **delusional thinking**, sidestepping reality in the vain pursuit of the unachievable. To which the motivationalists answer: anything is possible and, with application, effort and luck, you can reach your goals!

Yes, it is **possible**. But think about it: is it remotely **probable**?

Let's take an example. One of the great maxims of the self-actualisation movement is that anyone can grow up to be the president of the United States. Well, not strictly true: under the US constitution, only natural-born citizens of the USA can become president. There is a loophole that allows citizens naturalised at the time the constitution was adopted to stand for the office, but you'd have to be more than 200 years old, which means you wouldn't look too good on the tele, so no one would vote for you. Now, technically you could become a citizen, get elected to the federal legislature and force through a constitutional amendment allowing people born overseas to run for president—yes, that is possible but, honestly, is it likely?

Now look at the chances of someone who was actually born in the USA. Of the forty-three presidents who have served since 1781, all have been white male Christians, twenty-six of whom did time in the military. The first female president can't be too far away (ditto the second coming of Jesus) but, historically, your chances of sitting in the Oval Office if you have breasts or you're black, Jewish, Taoist, a gay pacifist or Ralph Nader are frankly pathetic. As I write, the population of the United States has just topped 300,000,002, with a net gain of one person every ten seconds; even in the unlikely—some would say miraculous—event of a level playing field, you're looking at starting odds of 1:300 million. Entry-level funding for a run at the primaries is at least $100 million and you need the backing of the party powerbrokers plus connections to one of two, possibly three, family political dynasties.

Yes, it's possible. Highly improbable.

## 20   Thinking you can become the President of the USA

## 21   Becoming the President of the USA in 2001

Let's look at an aspiration more within your line of sight. You're a salesperson for a national office supplies company. The boss organises a training seminar to improve the sales figures for the September quarter and brings in a motivational speaker to fire up the troops. At a pivotal moment, the speaker turns from his PowerPoint presentation and says: 'If you want it bad enough, people, you can be the top sales rep for not only the September quarter, but for every goddamn quarter in every goddamn year!'

Everybody whoops and makes a note on their folders: 'I can be top sales rep for quarter if I want it bad enuff.'

Oh, really? How many people are in the room? 120. How many can be the top sales rep?

One.

Congratulations, Mr Motivation—you've just created 119 future losers. He made the mistake that so many HIP do:

## 23  Using unsustainable metaphors like '110%' and 'You can do it!'

Don't confuse possibility with probability. Calculate the odds of success, acknowledge your limitations and set your plans towards something that is realistically achievable. You'll be pleasantly surprised by the results. Let's get the diagram looking like this:

Aspirations ⟶ ⬭

Limitations ⟶ ⬭

Or better still, like this:

Aspirations ⟶ ○

Limitations ⟶ ⬯

That has to be a win–win situation.

# ROLE MODELS FOR THE INEFFECTIVE

*Number 1*

THOMAS MIDGLEY JUNIOR, mechanical engineer and chemist, was born in Beaver Falls, Pennsylvania, in 1891. The son of an inventor, Thomas showed an uncanny ability throughout his life for discovering things that would have been better left hidden by the darkness of ignorance.

While working for a subsidiary of General Motors he discovered that the addition of tetra-ethyl lead to gasoline prevented 'knocking' in internal combustion engines. The company dubbed the product Ethyl, avoiding any mention of lead that might have discouraged a public eager to embrace the product.

And embrace it they did. Ethyl became a popular additive until nearly every engine in the world was being run on leaded fuel, with the resultant release of vast amounts of the poisonous element into the atmosphere. In December 1922 the American Chemical Society awarded Midgley the William H Nichols Medal in recognition of his fine work.

However, it was becoming apparent that Ethyl created a few problems. Many workers in the plants where the compound was produced began to experience hallucinations, insanity or death, and not always in that order. Midgley himself contracted lead poisoning and moved to Miami for the fresh air. Apparently it was fresher in those days. But he remained confident in his discovery—during a press conference to show how safe it was, Midgley poured liquid Ethyl over his hands and then inhaled it from a bottle for sixty seconds, maintaining he could do this every day and suffer no ill-effects. Prudently, he didn't repeat the experiment.

In 1930, GM charged Midgley with the job of finding a replacement for the volatile and dangerous chemicals that were then used in refrigerators. He discovered dichlorodifluoromethane, a chlorinated fluorocarbon (CFC) that became widely used in refrigerators, heat pumps, aerosol cans and asthma inhalers. Midgley called it freon, and was awarded the Perkins Medal in 1937 for the discovery that eventually led to the depletion of the ozone layer and potentially doomed life on earth to a slow death from ultra-violet radiation. In 1941, the American Chemical Society, unaware that freon would one day be banned by the Montreal Protocol, awarded Midgley its highest award, the Priestley Medal, and then followed it up with the William Gibbs Medal in 1942 for good measure.

Sadly, a nice display cabinet of medals could not prevent Midgley contracting polio at the age of fifty-one. Undaunted, he invented an elaborate contraption of ropes, levers and pulleys to manoeuvre himself in bed but tragically, at the age of fifty-five, he became entangled in it and strangled himself to death.

However, what was a sad day for the Midgley family was probably a happy one for the earth in general. One historian noted that Midgley 'had more impact on the atmosphere than any other single organism in history'. And I don't think he meant it in a nice way.

So which of the 700 habits was Midgley guilty of? Well, here's a few:

## 24  Ignoring constructive advice

Unable to accept the validity of scientific concern about his discovery, Midgley refused to believe Ethyl was dangerous. Either that or, confused by lead inhalation, he thought they were talking about his Aunt Ethel. And even there he got it wrong—she was a mean bitch who king-hit complete strangers.

## 25  Inventing environmentally disastrous pollutants

True. Sure, it's a niche category but they also manufacture un-earthed electrical appliances, choking-hazard toys and thalidomide.

## 26  Never knowing when to abandon a bad idea

In Midgley's case, he could have spared the world a lot of grief if he'd retired at the age of fourteen.

## 28  Trying to save money by doing it yourself

If he'd only hired professional rope/lever/pulley installers, Midgley would have lived to witness the damage he wrought. And we could've sued the bastard.

# 4
# THE TOP TEN

'Try as hard as we may for perfection, the net result of
our labours is an amazing variety of imperfectness. We are
inspired at our own versatility in being able to fail in so many
different ways.'
*Samuel McChord Crothers*

This page is copyright. Do not replicate without permission.

I'd never heard of him either.

Now by this stage in the book, you may be tired or confused. It may be some months since you read the preceding pages, or perhaps you flipped straight to the last page of the book to see how it ends. You may have only just rediscovered it after finally getting rid of that table with one short leg. In any case, I think you're ready for a summary, because you're probably the sort of person who doesn't handle detail well.

And that's not something to be ashamed of. It's pathetic, but not shameful. It's human nature to seek the quick fix because detail and elaboration are time-consuming, require effort and are often confusing. How many self-improvement books have you bought and flicked through looking for the silver bullets, the short and memorable tips for a better life? How often have you been disappointed? You've probably forgotten, because your short-, medium- and long-term memory are hopelessly inadequate. But, please, try to remember this: there are no shortcuts to success, except those handed out randomly to lucky bastards by a fickle universe that doesn't even know you exist. And they won't be coming your way.

So, if you're one of those people who think a *Reader's Digest* abridged novelette is still way too long, here are the Top Ten Habits of Highly Ineffective People:

1 **Procrastinating**

2 **Lacking organisational skills**

3 **Ignoring history**

4 **Thinking you can have it all**

5 **Neither acknowledging nor methodically refuting criticism**

6 **Having no sense of your own limitations**

7 **Not being able to communicate**

8 **Worrying**

9 **Living in fear of disappointing—or being disappointed**

10 **Forgetting to water the pot plants.**

Yes, that last one is a surprise—I've never seen it as a serious obstacle to a productive life but it's symptomatic of the myriad details that the ineffective ignore at their peril. Of course there are others—690 in fact—and many of them can have fairly serious effects on your lifestyle, like …

29 **Contracting fatal diseases**

But these ten are more than enough for most people to cope with in a lifetime of disappointment. So now we'll take a longer look at the first on the list: procrastination.

But before we do that, why don't we make some marmalade?

## *Ineffective Marmalade*

First up, you need some Seville oranges. Plant orange trees in well drained, lightly mulched soil and grow to maturity, usually three to five years, then pick fruit. Alternatively, for a more immediately available marmalade, go to your local fruit shop and buy some oranges—and you don't need to go to Seville. Slice the oranges thinly, removing all the pips and the stringy bit in the middle. Simmer in water with salt; for one kilo of fruit, allow 3.658 litres of water and half a teaspoon of salt (teaspoons are the little ones)—until soft. Rest in a ceramic bowl for 24 hours—the fruit, that is, not yourself.

Next day, or whenever you get around to it, measure fruit and water into a large pan and bring to the boil, adding a cup of sugar for every cup of fruit and water. Return to the boil for 25 minutes until set. Then bottle in hot sterilised jars. Wrap pointless doilies around lids, write 'Homemade Olde Marmalade' on labels, then distribute as unwanted Christmas gifts.

# To Do Lists

## The Effective:

1 Make final mortgage payment (Tuesday).

2 Book restaurant for mortgage celebration dinner for two (!)

3 Revise CV for next week's promotion interview with CJ—send CJ's husband golf package vouchers. Retain receipt for tax deduction.

4 Liaise with real estate agent over new tenants for investment property.

5 Frame Thank You certificate from the village of Nga-hi-sotu for new schoolhouse and goat herd.

6 Finish advisory paper to UN on North Korea options.

7 Renew subscriptions to ballet, symphony and experimental performance company.

8 Install base station for wireless internet in guest wing.

9 Revise Sanskrit for semester exam.

10 Book stretch limo for Liberti's Year 5 farewell.

11 Send flowers to thank my special lady for extra special night!

12 Make time for me.

## The Ineffective:

1. Find car.
2. Fix leaking downpipe nr back door.
3. Replace water damaged back door.
4. Fill out guarantee for TV we got three years ago. HIGH PRIORITY
5. Reschedule appointment with bank manager.
6. Finish off skirting boards and architraves in sunroom.
7. Buy Dad birthday present for last year or at least send 'Whoops!' card.
8. Finish off walls and ceiling in sunroom.
9. Stop drinking on week nights.
10. Consolidate super funds. Put more into super. Cut out takeaways on week nights.
11. Play with kids no matter what they say.
12. Remember wedding anniversary this year.
13. Revise career options – must be something else I can do.

# 5
# WHAT'S THE RUSH?

'Procrastination is the thief of time.'
*Edward Young*

The word *procrastinate* comes from the Latin *pro crastinare*, meaning literally 'of tomorrow'. In reality, it usually means 'of next month. Or never'. A recent US survey showed that 20 per cent of respondents regarded themselves as chronic procrastinators—and that figure was only calculated from the number of people who actually got around to filling in the form. All found the condition caused stress, anxiety and a feeling of inadequacy, not to mention a lot of library fines for overdue books.

## 30 Putting off until tomorrow what you should have done yesterday

The underlying causes of procrastination are many and varied, usually behavioural, although some scientists now believe that there may be a physiological reason for it.

Primarily, this theory revolves around a malfunctioning pre-frontal cortex (PFC), which is that part of the brain's frontal lobe that deals with everyday functions such as judgement, planning, critical thinking and attention span.

A fully functioning PFC sends signals to the sensory and limbic parts of the brain (whatever they are) and when there is a need for mental focus, it filters out distracting input from the other regions of the cerebrum. A PFC fully on the job can give you that wonderful feeling of being 'lost in concentration' by blocking out extraneous sensory stimuli. On the other hand, a PFC that's basically cactus can lead to the extremes of attention deficit disorder and associated conditions. It's possible that a trait (or habitual) procrastinator may have a damaged PFC. Or they might get round to getting one eventually.

Far more likely is that the problem is psychological, stemming from a fear of failure (or even success), a lack of optimism or self-belief, or the need to shift blame. Or maybe you simply couldn't be less interested. Laboratory tests have shown that procrastination is a behavioural self-handicap only when the task was deemed evaluative. In other words, you only delay doing something of importance that will eventually be judged by others. Pointless tasks present no problem: no one has ever said 'I won't sit on my fat arse now, I'll sit on it tomorrow.'

Joseph Ferrari, Associate Professor of Psychology at De Paul University in Chicago, identifies three main types of procrastinator:

## 1. THE AROUSAL TYPE

Not as exciting as it sounds; this is the sort of person who leaves things to the last minute and then experiences a rush of emotion when the job is finally done.

## 2. THE AVOIDER

Motivated by a fear of the opinions of others—would rather be seen to have failed due to lack of effort, rather than lack of talent. The 'Oh, if only I'd had more time I could have easily done it' people.

## 3. THE DECISIONAL PROCRASTINATOR

Endlessly researching options, unable to make a decision, thus absolving themselves of responsibility for the outcome of events. The sort of person who finally embraces a new technology three days before it becomes obsolete.

## 31 Being easily categorised on an index of failure

Identifying procrastination tendencies is easy; the hard part is overcoming them. Any number of books have been written over the years on the subject and some of them have even been published. Essentially they involve lists, action plans and prioritisation strategies, which all worked fine for the Nazis but aren't going to do a lot for someone who would rather re-sharpen their satay skewers than tackle that assignment, or sales schedule or whatever equally vital job they've got to finish.

New approaches are needed. Professor John Perry, a philosopher at Stanford University, suggests 'structured procrastination'. Don't reduce the number of things you have to do because you won't even do the reduced workload. Instead, place a task of relatively high importance at the top of your To Do list.

## 32 Having either 58 To Do lists or none

Ideally, it should be a task that will take several years to complete, like writing a screenplay or restoring that rotting boat you found on the kerb in the council clean-up. Next, peel eight limes and watch the third series of *Seinfeld*. Then place more important and pressing tasks further down the list. Theoretically, you'll get around to those jobs, having mentally tricked yourself that the number one job can wait.

Not convinced? Hardly surprising. Then try this simple plan: allot ten minutes—and ten minutes only—to a task. Set a timer and don't go a second over. Repeat three times a day. Gradually increase either the allotted time or the number of repeats, breaking the task up into achievable subsets. (This is an approach based on the maxim that the longest journey begins with the first step—equally, it ends with the last but it's the sort of psycho-motivational drivel that your ancient Chinese philosophers couldn't churn out fast enough.) If it's a university assignment, say, the first ten minutes might be spent on the title; the second on Googling an appropriate essay to plagiarise and the third devoted to downloading same. Or if your task is outside the home, give yourself the first ten minutes to get to the job, the second to prepare tools and the third to pack up and leave.

If you fall into the Arousal category—those who put things off until the last minute—here's a radical solution. Put **everything** off until the last minute. If you have to wake up at 6.30 a.m. for an important appointment, don't go to sleep until 6.25. If you're feeling peckish, don't eat anything until you collapse. Then see how much you like it.

The serial Avoider fears the judgement of others. Ask yourself this: what do they already think of me? Is it going to get any worse if my work is inadequate? Probably not; they might possibly think more of you if you actually do something, even if your sales strategy has only one bullet point that says 'Increase sales'. It's short, it's to the point and the average management executive should be able to absorb it in a single reading. Position yourself as a big-picture, blue-sky creative type and leave the detail to others. Believe me, whole careers have been built on this approach.

The Decisional Procrastinator is in a fast-growing category, largely due to modern society's obsession with choice. Time was when you simply had the phone put on; there was one company offering one option and if you wanted to be connected, you simply applied. Six months later, you were given a phone that worked for three days and then you waited another six months for a replacement. It wasn't ideal, and perhaps your father-in-law would still be alive today if you'd been able to get through to the ambulance, but at least the decision was taken out of your hands. These days, the number of communication options available to you would fill a phone book. Months can be spent researching the most cost-effective plan; a modern phone has multiple functions completely unrelated to telephony—like storing more pictures than the Louvre and sending MP3 files to Mongolia—and is invariably obsolete by the time you've recycled the packaging. You then have to program the wretched thing, firewire your address book into it and set the GPS co-ordinates while giving yourself cancer of the brain every time some call centre in India rings up to offer you a new service plan.

Similarly, if you subscribe to consumer *Choice* magazine and do some background reading on LCD TVs, the recommended model is only available on back-order and is incompatible with your existing power supply, aerial and/or the DVD/hard drive/wax cylinder recording device you bought duty free in Suva. Not to mention that when you've finally enlisted an electronic engineer to install it there's nothing worth watching and the sub-woofer on your home cinema system smells like burning toast every time you turn it on.

The moral to be learnt here is: don't waste precious time on consumer research. Walk into the nearest shop, point to an appliance you like the look of and say 'I'll have that one please.' (Obviously, make sure you're in the right shop; there's no point in asking for a reverse cycle air-conditioner in an organic butchery.) Why bother fact finding when you know disappointment and frustration are inevitable anyway, no matter how much cost comparison and service reliability ranking you do? You know in the pit of your stomach that the phone plan you just signed up to for two years is going to cost twice as much as one offered the next day. It's written in stone that the laptop you buy—recommended by *Wired*, *Your PC* and *Which Notebook?*—is going to freeze as soon as you turn it on and have half the capability of a handheld Ninjungai gaming console that hit the stores overnight in Tokyo.

Whatever decision you make, it's going to be compromised within minutes. Get over it and take pot luck like the rest of us.

What's the Rush?

# PROCRASTINATOR'S FLOW CHART

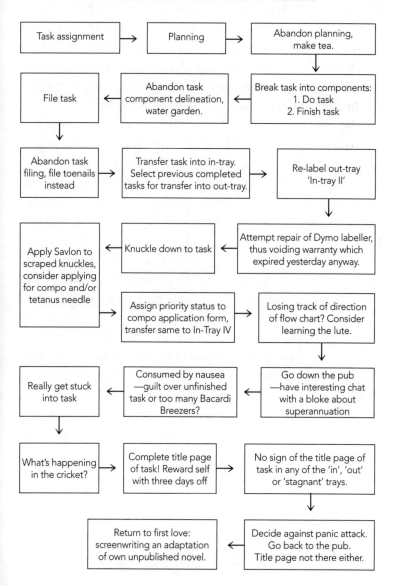

# 6
# FEAR OF DISAPPOINTMENT

'The disappointment of manhood succeeds the disillusion of youth.'
*Benjamin Disraeli*

This page may be kept as a useful gift tag.

For the ineffective, the fear of being disappointed—or worse, disappointing others—shadows their lives. But by seeking to avoid it they risk missing out on the potential satisfaction of achievement, however humble—that bright golden thread that weaves beguilingly through the rich tapestry of our lives. For disappointment is one of those tedious, black/white contrasting emotions that allows you to experience joy or euphoria. Without disappointment, there can be no hope. Without failure, there can be no success; without defeat, no victory unless you're extremely good at everything.

Let's imagine a debriefing after a project that has fallen through. Which of the following statements do you most identify with?

### STATEMENT A:

'Look, I know we're all disappointed but this is nothing more than a reality check. We'd put the work in, we had every chance of succeeding but sadly, on the day, we didn't succeed. Let's learn from this, move on and try again.'

## STATEMENT D:

'I knew this would happen but would anyone listen to me? I mean, why do we bother? Is there anything we can do right—you wouldn't think so, on the strength of this debacle, would you? You just watch, someone's going to be copping the blame and what's the bet it's going to be me? That'd be so typical. Why should today be any different? Yes, thank you God for yet another dismal twenty-four hours on the planet. I just wanted *something* to go well but no, you couldn't see your way to that, not even the once. Thanks again for nothing. Not that I'm blaming you. I know: it's me. My life is shit. And … oh, great! My fly is undone. Thanks for telling me guys—no, no, why should today be any different …?'

If you chose Statement D, you probably don't cope well with disappointment. But it's not a complete disappointment—at least you identify the problem.

'We express disappointment in everything but ourselves,' observed the American aphorist Mason Cooley. In other words, we usually try to shift the blame somewhere else and refuse to acknowledge our own shortcomings. Not only that, the truly ineffective go one step further and also tend to do the reverse, blaming themselves for everything that has, will, or could possibly go wrong.

### 34 Not accepting responsibility for your actions

### 35 Accepting too much responsibility for your actions

Too easily you can become the fall guy for other people's failures. Try to realistically assign your proportion of responsibility in anything that goes wrong by considering the problem from the perspective of all concerned. Because thinking 'It's all my fault' is a tacit admission that there's nothing you can (or are prepared to) do to fix the problem. It's almost as bad as refusing to accept any responsibility at all. By accepting less of the overall responsibility, the problem may not seem so overwhelming and you'll be more able to make amends.

## 36   Having too much riding on the outcome of everything you do

## 37   Setting yourself up to be inevitably disappointed

This can be done in a number of ways. Firstly, by raising the bar of expectation so high it can never be reached. For some people this almost becomes a psychosis. The actor Peter Sellers suffered terribly from this condition—everything he bought, worked on or even fell in love with failed to live up to the unreasonable expectations he'd invested in it. An avaricious consumer, he always bought the latest car, gadget or technology but invariably found it wanting within days of purchase. Cars would be returned because a tiny rattle had developed; a hi-fi system sent back because a slight hiss could be heard in one corner of the room at a certain volume. His personal relationships all suffered for the same reason; his children were a major disappointment to him and he would punish them, often quite ruthlessly, simply because they weren't exactly what he wanted them to be. Why do people behave in this self-destructive manner? I have no idea. Equally, I have no idea why he made *The Secret Cabinet of Fu Manchu*—it was rubbish.

Equally damaging is expecting disappointment, even when the bar of expectation is set at ankle height. Negative wish fulfilment is linked to a fear of success, which itself is linked to a desire to escape the evaluative judgement of others. Too easy to say: if I habitually anticipate failure then habitually fail, all has gone just as I (and everyone else) predicted. All our expectations have been reached.

It also absolves you of the need to make any effort—why bother if it's not going to work anyway? Not having made an effort, any potential fruits of your efforts cannot be judged. Nor can they be ridiculed. Philip Dormer Stanhope, the 4th Earl of Chesterfield, observed: 'There is always a degree of ridicule that attends a disappointment, though often very unjustly, if the expectation was reasonably grounded; however, it is certainly most prudent not to communicate, prematurely, one's hopes or fears.'

Of course, he's absolutely right, that's why he was an Earl of Chesterfield—they don't hand out those things to just anybody. And his words suggest a strategy to break the cycle.

Allow yourself ten victories a day. Keep them modest (*reasonably grounded*) and keep them private—others may not share your triumph in the successful sharpening of a pencil to find that the lead doesn't break off two minutes later. You will gradually learn, through the pride in small achievements, that not everything has to end in disillusion and futility. Life does, but that's another matter.

## 38  Living in fear of being duped

A corollary of disappointment, the fear of being duped or tricked can lead to excessive caution bordering on timidity.

Don't automatically assume that everyone is out to get you simply because most of them are. The gift of trust is one that you should welcome, despite the responsibilities it brings—why not return the gift of it to others? Of course, the tricky part is determining who deserves it but it is better to occasionally fail in the attempt than never attempt it at all. The character lessons you learn as you hand over your life savings to what seemed a perfectly legitimate bank in Nigeria or you watch your fridge being wheeled away by that nice repairman you met in the street will hold you in good stead for your future dealings with the wider world.

## 39   Fearing the disappointment of others

Ineffective people are often rendered so by their responses to the perceived attitudes of others. Often these attitudes don't even exist—the ineffective are very poor judges of character and mood. The fear of being judged negatively by those around you can have a paralysing result, rendering you incapable of any positive action. The level of anxiety over possibly disappointing others usually correlates with the circles of influence in your life: your family, your friends, your colleagues, each circle slowly diminishing in significance until you finally reach people you've never met. The fear of letting down Julia Roberts or Nelson Mandela may be real to you, but it's relatively unlikely to eventuate.

It's difficult to say 'Who cares what they think?' but there comes a time when all of us need to say just that. Pick your time carefully—avoid pressure moments like a court appearance, job interview or an audience with the Pope. To begin with, try to project your newfound self-confidence to someone in an outer circle of influence. If you're suddenly engaged in a conversation with a call centre in Bangalore, it's the perfect opportunity for positive self-assertion. Put out of your mind those cautionary thoughts, those mental roadblocks like 'Perhaps he's got a point and I do need an increased credit limit with no extra charges' or 'He's only doing his job and what if he loses it? He's probably supporting his family and they're suffering terribly in the drought in the Punjab'. Then firmly, yet politely, put the phone down.

Or if you sense encouragement from others in a decision-making situation, don't be afraid to run with it. There are appropriate environments for possible failure, and a sympathetic mentor can ease you through the most difficult of tests. If they say 'I take my tea however it comes' they probably mean it, so don't stress about how much milk to put in or the fact that you're serving Irish Breakfast in the afternoon.

## 40  Relying on other people for your happiness

## 41  Being constantly disappointed in other people

You're forgetting that they're probably fearing this very result (see above) and may not be at their scintillating best. Contrary to popular belief, every person is essentially an island. Occasionally bridges or causeways are extended to others but these are in constant need of repair and even then they can fall away into the sea of existential despair. Or the other islands might just get sick of you. People usually fail to meet our expectations simply because we ask too much of them. Expect less and you'll be pleasantly surprised when you get more.

## 42   Not using disappointment constructively

It's going to happen, so learn to use it. While it's destructive to be constantly let down by other people, occasionally you can use it to your advantage. Employed benevolently, with an understanding sigh and a shake of the head, expressing disappointment in others may inspire them to greater efforts in the future. Shamed by their failure to satisfy your needs, they may redouble their resolve.

## 43   Failing to recognise that disappointment breeds hope

Never forget that the beauty of disappointment is that it gives you a wonderful opportunity to be disappointed all over again.

## ROLE MODELS FOR THE INEFFECTIVE

*Number 2*

HAMLET PRINCE OF DENMARK was born in Elsinore and studied at the University of Wittenberg with his second-best friends Rosencrantz and Guildenstern, president and social secretary of the university Gay Danes Society. Early childhood influences included court jester Yorrick, best friend Horatio, and his father the king, Hamlet Snr. Some scholars also suggest a strong Oedipal bond with his mother Gertrude, although that probably says more about them than Hamlet.

When Hamlet returned from study leave, the ghost of his father appeared on the battlements and told him that his uncle Claudius, now married to Gertrude, had poisoned him in the orchard. Hamlet resolved to avenge his father's death but because there were another four acts to go, he decided to take things slowly.

First up, he arranged for some strolling players to re-enact his father's death, hoping to force a confession from his uncle. Like that was going to work! Falling back on Plan B, he offended his friend Laertes by sending Ophelia, Laertes's sister, stark raving mad. She was last seen floating face down in a stream and Hamlet made matters worse by stabbing her father, Polonius, to death behind the arras.

Meanwhile, Claudius sent Rosencrantz and Guildenstern to accompany Hamlet to England, knowing full well that it was all but impossible for Hamlet to get a working visa in the UK. Worse still, he sent a letter in their overnight luggage asking the King of England to kill the Danish prince. Hamlet discovered the letter and, understandably upset, despatched his two friends to inevitable death in his place, nipping back to Denmark to finish off his uncle.

Laertes, now back at home on study leave, got wind of what had been going on. Hard to avoid it, really, with his father and sister both dead. But, being emotionally drained, he was easily recruited by Claudius to kill Hamlet in a rigged fencing duel. Claudius poisoned the sword tip and, for good measure, poisoned the sports drink that Hamlet would drink during the breaks.

Now, you're not going to believe what happened next: Gertrude accidentally drank the laced Gatorade and Laertes stabbed Hamlet with the poisoned sword but before the plucky prince hit the deck, he managed to take out both Laertes and Claudius. Horatio, arriving home on study leave, found a castle full of corpses and the Norwegian Fortinbras banging on the kingdom's door looking to take over the place. Have it, said Horatio, and he went back to Wittenberg where he switched to a post-graduate degree in hospitality.

Where to begin with Hamlet's bad habits …?

## 44  Putting off until tomorrow what you should do today

The big one. If a ghost appears on a battlement saying 'Avenge my death!', you've got to action his proposal as top priority. Don't e-mail everyone else to see if it's a good idea; just get on with it, preferably in a bloodlust. This is not the sort of thing you should sleep on. Mind you, Hamlet reminds us of the typical child: you've got to yell at them a million times before they do any one simple thing you ask them to.

## 45  Killing the wrong people

How often do we see that happen? It is so wrong, people. Revenge only works if you pick the right target. There is no point in killing someone who jilted someone else's sister; it has to be **your** sister. Hamlet was after one guy—he winds up indirectly killing seven! Poor planning, poor execution. Literally.

## 46  Believing actors can change the world

'The play's the thing in which I'll catch the conscience of the king,' says Hamlet after asking a bunch of strolling thespians to perform a short synopsis he's been working on. Everyone's writing a script! Frankly, Hamlet's cunning plan is going to have as much impact as Susan Sarandon wearing a black armband to the Oscars—or worse, the BAFTAs. Don't think for a minute that a celebrity's opinions are any better thought out than yours. It's just that they are famous, you are not. Their garbage bins are more interesting than yours for the same reason.

# 7

# COMMUNICATION, OR GETTING WHAT YOU WANT TO SAY OVER IN THE BEST SORT-OF, LIKE, WAY POSSIBLE

'Ambition is the last refuge of the failure.'
*Oscar Wilde*

This page is for you—because you're special.

For a huge blouse who died penniless at the age of forty-six, Oscar Wilde knew a thing or two about the human condition. Look at this quote from *The Importance of Being Earnest*:

> Miss Prism: *You must remember his constant anxiety about that unfortunate young man his brother.*
>
> *Act Two, Scene 1*

Delicious, isn't it? But then most gays are witty, at least on TV. Still, they don't write them like that these days. In fact, too many people are guilty of:

## 47 Not being able to spell

## 49 Having no understanding of grammar

## 50 txtng nsted of ritng

These are all symptoms of a widening malaise in the modern world: a general inability to communicate. It's said that a picture is worth a thousand words, which is the sort of meaningless aphorism that makes my eyes water. But like all clichés it does contain a modicum of truth. However, what actually separates the human species from the rest of the animal kingdom (apart from deodorant and microwave popcorn) is an ability to verbalise.

We don't actually do pictures very well. Let's face it, a baboon with learning difficulties could draw just as well as the average human being. Artistic talent is yet another thing in which most of us are profoundly deficient. (Note that I didn't end the sentence with the preposition—that's the sort of attention to linguistic detail I'm speaking of.) Most of us can't even take a decent photo. Given our propensity to render our friends and loved ones as headless blurs and then e-mail them to others—like they're interested!—it's vital that we retain and exercise our capacity for verbal and written communication. Too often we avoid it. Haven't we all been secretly grateful to hear an answering machine when making a social duty phone call to 'touch base'?

## 51  Using annoying phrases like 'touch base'

Even worse, to avoid actually having to speak to the person, we send text messages. Texting is often defended by post-modernist lecturers in media studies as a new way of writing, a linguistic revolution. Wot a bnch of wnkaz. And of whom I simply ask: if speech-to-text-recognition software were available in our handsets, how many of us would stand like slack-jawed gibbons punching tiny keys with our thumbs? Exit the post-modernists, shamefaced! But have they, in a real sense, gone or is that merely a subjective construct?

## 52  Being post-modernist

Not surprisingly, our real communications skills—one-on-one human interaction—get rusty. It may be useful to determine what has led us to this point of aversion to human dialogue. Not being a sociologist or psychologist, I have little knowledge of the subject but since when has that been a reason to not have an opinion?

I believe it's symptomatic of our increasing self-centredness. The communal experiences of the past—village life, public transport, the theatre or cinema, orgies, etc.—have been replaced by the air-conditioned car, the plasma screen watched alone, replays and online erotica. As society fragments into its smallest constituent parts (individuals) it becomes harder to reassemble the group, except in times of natural disaster, when people revert to their instinctive need to collectively loot, blame the government or rort insurance companies.

This fragmentation manifests itself in any number of ineffective habits …

## 53  Thinking the art of conversation is waiting for your turn to speak

Conversation is an interactive and evolutionary process whose direction should be dictated by what is being said, rather than simply becoming an interchange of prepared statements or points of view. What you say should ideally be influenced by what you've just heard but too often we have no idea of what the other person is actually talking about and even less interest, merely leaping in with our two bob's worth whenever they stop to draw breath. Drawing on a wide range of meaningless subjects, conversation is continuously degraded to small talk, what the linguists call phatic communication, where the action of speaking at all becomes more important than what is being said. Popular topics are the weather, sport and the personal lives of minor celebrities.

Usually, these subjects that we inanely banter back and forth are determined by the mass media; the very mention of the words 'Kate Moss', for example, provokes a series of preconceived responses that reflects the agenda set out in the gossip magazines. Does any of us know Kate Moss? Hardly. The conversation can proceed, safe in the knowledge that thought will not be required and we can drop in or out of consciousness at any point yet still know exactly what's being said.

This concept of regurgitative dialogue even has its own name: 'water cooler' discussion. Apparently, the surest sign that a topic has entered the cultural zeitgeist is when it is talked about by persons standing around a device for chilling and dispensing water. Sociologists are unsure whether the habit has spread to cultures in the developing world; is there 'stand-pipe' discussion in India, for example, or 'stagnant bore' chat in drought stricken Darfur? What will we do for cultural interaction when global warming has rendered the water cooler a redundant luxury?

Try beginning a conversation with a workmate on an unrelated subject. Offer a subjective point of view and encourage them to respond to it, listening carefully to their thoughts on the topic. Agree or disagree with their position and then advance the discussion by proposing an alternative thesis, drawing on examples from your own personal experience or facts you've gleaned from extensive reading of current journals and periodicals. When your conversation colleague's eyes glaze over, suggest an iced water and a chat about Pamela Anderson's breast augmentation, or 'rack pack'.

## 54 Thinking gossip is socially therapeutic

There's a fashionable belief that gossip is in some way good for society, that it breaks down class distinctions and oils human interaction, deflating envy and aggression as the have-nots harmlessly vent their resentment against the haves. It's a false belief largely perpetuated by those with a stake in gossip magazines that have spread like a cancer throughout western societies. Of course, gossips have been with us since humans first lived together in groups—there was always some Neanderthal bitching about another cave-dweller because his pelt was bigger or less moth-eaten or whatever. Noah refused gossips access to the ark, but he took cockroaches, warthogs and pubic lice; the man had some taste.

For its practitioners, the beauty of gossip is that it requires no substantiation or first-hand knowledge. In fact, the more fanciful it is, the better. Its value rises with its level of maliciousness—it's surprising how easily people will believe the worst of others. The internet and the rise of the blog (vanity publishing of the electronic age) have ushered in a new age of vitriol, with the perpetrators hiding behind a wall of digital anonymity. The destructiveness of gossip, allied as it is to innuendo and smear, has spread into almost every aspect of society, degrading the political process and our civic institutions. Its abrasive force has been professionally harnessed by push-pollsters, focus groups and negative advertisement campaigning and repeatedly used to fog the truth on any number of issues. And it's not until you've been on the receiving end of gossip that you realise how painful it can be.

Simple solution: ignore it. Don't listen to it, don't spread it. Take a look at the people around you and figure out exactly where gossip gets them. Nowhere.

## 55  Mistaking interactive TV polls for social participation

I'm sure the introduction of cable television has lead to many benefits but I can't think of any offhand. Still, one of its more promising aspects has been the introduction of interactive polling, where the viewer can register a yes/no response to pressing social issues of the day, like 'Should gay marriage be allowed?' or 'Is Hilary Duff hot?' So far, a button to register 'Possibly, but I need to examine the issues more comprehensively' has proved beyond technological capabilities.

This over-simplification of debate and the apparent ease of entering the civic discourse has made it possible for lethargic, couch-oriented citizens to believe they can alter the direction of government. Even worse, it's possible that they do, with poll-driven politicians now thinking that long-range forward-planning means what's happening next Friday, and busily poring over the results of any straw poll conducted on talkback radio or in the back bar of The Cricketer's Arms.

Having pressed the appropriate button on their remote controls, the lard-arsed smugly nod when 96 per cent of those surveyed support their position, little knowing that the figure represents twenty-four of the twenty-five fellow losers who bothered to vote. If you think Rupert Murdoch wants your opinion, deliver it a little more forcefully, preferably where it stings.

## 57 Sending online greeting cards

Is there a limper way of expressing the joy you feel on the anniversary of someone's birth than sending an online greeting, where the thought and effort required is all of a few keystrokes and a flick of the mouse? No thoughtful selection in the local card shop of a clever Far Side cartoon or a retro photo of old people with some hilariously inappropriate double entendre here. No sweating over the wording of the witty accompanying message, no trudging up the road to buy a stamp and post the bloody thing. Just some ghastly Microsoft animation of streamers and balloons waving to the tinny rendering of 'Happy Birthday' on an electronic instrument that sounds like a blowfly being repeatedly hit about the head. If you can't be bothered going to some sort of trouble, don't bother at all.

## 58 Sending an annual form letter via e-mail to friends and family

If I could tear e-mails of this sort out of the computer and rip them up, I would. It really makes you feel worthwhile receiving news of a friend when you realise he's sent exactly the same affectionate greetings to 238 other people, including his netbanking facility and service provider. Tedious details of what the kids have done, where they went on their holiday and the discount rate they got on the room and airport transfer, the demise of a pet you've never met and the comforting reassurance that they'll be thinking of you when they pop a bubbly on Christmas Day ... They could pop an aortic valve and you'd feel nothing.

If you insist on using this method of non-communication, either because you've left it all too late and UNICEF or the Society of Foot and Mouth Artists ran out of cards, at least try to disguise the fact that you think so little of the people you're sending it to. Tick the Undisclosed Recipients preference; use some sort of mail-merge program that allows you to personalise aspects of the letter; and, to give it that nice personal touch, add an anecdote that only a few on your list will recognise, like:

'Hey, remember that nasty rash I got on the walking tour of New Zealand all those years ago? Crazy days! It's finally healed up, thank goodness, so now we can use the bar stools we got from the Ikea clearance centre for less than half price!'

Just make sure you send the right anecdote to the right people.

## 59 Forwarding online 'jokes'

Despite the fact that we're sinking in a sea of information, there are people sitting in darkened rooms all over the globe manufacturing even more bad jokes, funny pictures and goofy animations to add to the daily stream of garbage that we now must filter through. The information age has unleashed a torrent of text and images as if in a scene from 'The Sorcerer's Apprentice', a self-replicating miasma of pointlessness that threatens to drown us all. But unlike dear old Mickey, we don't have a benign wizard to come home and undo the spell. (Younger readers may like to refer to a history of Disney animation at this point. Ancient readers may even remember the original folk tale before the mouse got involved.)

## Communication

Please think twice before hitting the Forward button. Is that picture of George W Bush with his head up Cheney's backside really going to make the day of everyone in your address book, including your net-banking facility and service provider?

Even this short selection of bad habits highlights a central problem: we're not sure what communicating means any more. Technology has elevated the simple exchange of information to equate with communication. But ironically, the more information we get, the less we understand. Picture a river meeting the sea—come on, visualise! We're supposed to be good at it! The narrow, fast moving current once cut a deep and indelible canyon. But the wider the spreading delta, the shallower and shallower it gets, until it begins to clog with silt and debris. Right now the world is ankle deep in muddy, tepid water. The information superhighway has gone the way of all highways: no sooner have you built eight lanes than they've filled with traffic and ground to a halt. More roads simply create more and more traffic, until you'd be quicker walking.

One of the so-called express lanes of the information superhighway is e-mail, that great revolution of the promised paperless office—now there's an oxymoron. In mid-2006, the Ironport spam filtering service estimated that nine out of ten e-mails sent over the internet were unsolicited junk mail. But there's an even more insidious downside to the e-mail revolution. Because it's simple to keep *everybody* in the loop on a project, we all get dragged in. This culture of inclusion leads to diminished self-reliance, a paranoid need to cover your back, to share the responsibility among as many scapegoats as possible. Personal initiative and decisive judgements suffer as fear of collective finger-pointing leaves no one willing to accept the consequences of possible error. Whatever happened to 'nothing ventured, nothing gained'? Columbus would still be sitting in Spain if he'd had to e-mail every department to give them a heads-up and keep them all on the same page about the Americas project.

## 60 Letting technology dictate your life

Technology has given us a great licence to do, well, pretty much anything. What it doesn't do is give us the judgement to know if we should. Simply because the technological opportunity presents itself don't automatically assume that you should take it. Is it going to complicate or simplify your life? Will it end up being yet another thing to maintain, monitor and pay for? Can you do the same task with a pencil?

Here's a good example. One of the greatest cons of the digital age has been the PDA, the Personal Digital Assistant, a hand-held computing device that provides e-mail, internet, phone, media player, contact databases and spread sheets. More often than not, they're sold with promise of the flexibility and 'freedom' to work from home—or even on the beach, the ads filled with happy business executives in Greg Norman golf shirts lying in hammocks tapping on their Blackberries as their kids build sandcastles. The myth is that this form of telecommuting gives you more free time, but in fact the reverse is true: work becomes the constant shadow darkening your life, and your loyalty to the corporate cause is measured by your willingness to be on call seven days a week. Work ceases to be a finite aspect of the way you live, a means to an end that can be compartmentalised and balanced with the other priorities of your life (i.e. having a life) and becomes instead the central and only focus. And that's even for those people without ambition, those who have little desire to make it all the way to the top. These days it's a bare-knuckle fight just to get to the middle.

## ROLE MODELS FOR THE INEFFECTIVE

*Number 3*

GENERAL GEORGE ARMSTRONG CUSTER was born in New Rumley, Ohio, in 1839 and as a young boy he hankered to be a soldier, despite labouring under the nicknames of Fanny and Yellow Hair. Still, it could have been worse: it might have been Yellow Fanny Hair. His childhood dream of militarism was fulfilled when he graduated from the US Military Academy in 1861, coming thirty-fourth in a class of thirty-four. His careers adviser should have started ringing the alarm bells even then but the American Civil War had just begun and much to everyone's surprise, Custer proved himself a reckless and fearless cavalry leader. His self-confidence enabled him to survive two court-martials, one for being absent without leave.

At the age of twenty-three he was appointed to the temporary rank of brigadier general and two years later he was made a major general. He also earned himself the dubious honour of being the most-photographed officer in the army. Already his robust ego was beginning to affect his judgement—he liked nothing better than sitting in front of a camera, his long hair coiled into ringlets sprinkled with cinnamon scented oil, wearing figure-hugging olive corduroy trousers, a sailor's shirt with silver stars on the collar, a red cravat and a black velveteen jacket. And that was just day wear.

Many of his colleagues envied his early success and resented his love of the limelight, but in a war-weary nation Custer's flamboyance made him a hero in the victorious North. At war's end in 1865, he was dropped back to captain and went off to fight the Indian Wars with the Seventh Cavalry Regiment. He would regularly invite press reporters along with him on various military actions; some say that he harboured secret ambitions to stand for the presidency.

Throughout the early 1870s, Custer led sorties in Montana and Dakota, announcing the discovery of gold in the Black Hills (formerly the Them Thar Hills) and skirmishing with the Native Americans, who were then being herded onto the reservations to open the land up for white settlers. In 1875, he smoked a peace pipe with the Lakota and swore he would never fight the Indians (that being the nomenclature of the times) again.

Little did they know he had his fingers crossed, because in June 1876, despite orders that he was to locate the Native Americans and await the arrival of an infantry column, Custer foolishly led his cavalry into the disastrous battle of Little Big Horn. Heavily outnumbered, he split his forces into three. One group, led by Major Marcus Reno, failed in its attempt to trap the enemy in a classic pincer movement; the other, led by Captain Frederick Benteen, rode about vaguely, seemingly unaware of what a classic pincer movement looked like, leaving Custer and his few hundred men surrounded on a hill, where they were slaughtered to the last man.

Two of Custer's brothers, Thomas and Boston, as well as his brother-in-law and a nephew, were all killed in the battle. Thankfully, his mother had stayed at home. The only US cavalry survivor was a horse called Comanche, but it was so traumatised it was unable to reveal to the army board of enquiry much of what happened. Many Native American warriors, including Hairy Moccasin, Moving Robe Woman and Wooden Leg, survived to eventually tell their stories.

Custer's death split public opinion. To many he was a national hero; to others, an incompetent, vainglorious egotist who sacrificed his men in a doomed and reckless enterprise. His fellow commanders Reno and Benteen were accused of being heavy drinkers and their careers suffered after the defeat, although not as badly as Custer's. Even today, he has his supporters and detractors, but one thing's for certain: he was hopelessly inept at calculating the number of Native Americans lining up to have a go at him.

## 61 Ignoring the odds

Odds are calculated for a reason. If you're outnumbered five to one, unless you're up against Girl Guides with their arms tied behind their backs, your chances of having the crap beaten out of you are extremely good. Custer made the fatal error of ignoring the statistical likelihood of several thousand well-armed, mounted warriors being able to whip his corduroy ass. History has yet to finally reveal whether it was bloody-mindedness, vanity or an honest mistake.

## 62 Doing anything to get into the media

Custer was one of the first military celebrities. If he'd survived Little Big Horn, he'd have cleaned up on the celebrity speaker circuit, hammering out some kind of connection between fighting Injuns (that being the informal nomenclature of the time) and achieving your goals in sales. His vanity and thirst for publicity were legendary—on a per capita basis he'd have given Paris Hilton a run for her money for most magazine covers. Custer even had a reporter with him at the final battle, although sadly the journalist didn't get to file the story, being more chock full of arrows than St Sebastian at the time. Remember the old adage: empty vessels make the most noise. Why they feel the need to keep on making it is anyone's guess.

## 63   Getting the camera out at the drop of a hat

Live in the moment! Keep a mental picture of the occasion in your head, write a haiku, draw a quick sketch—even model the thing out of Play-Doh, just keep the camera in its case for once in your life!

## 64   Wearing figure-hugging corduroy

If you're Hugh Grant or the third Earl of Surry pumping pheasants full of lead shot, you can look good in corduroy. If you're not, don't even bother. And figure-hugging couture should never be attempted by the average man. But if you do feel the pathological need for a fabric that moves like a second skin, stick to Lycra—and even then only in the privacy of your own home. Unless you've got abs cut like a draining board, safer to go for the generously tailored, loose-fitting or baggy apparel.

# 8
# IT'S A WORRY

'Anxiety is the poison of human life; the parent of many sins and of more miseries ... why this restless stir and commotion of mind? Can it alter the cause, or unravel the mystery of human events?'
*Tryon Edwards*

This page is a metaphor for life: largely pointless.

Elsewhere in this book we've heard about the impediments to effectiveness that shape the ineffective person. Somewhere within us all there is an effective person crying to get out— some can hear the call more strongly, others seem unaware of it altogether and may well go to their graves never knowing of the super-person that lurked deep inside their vitals. We build our own prisons, brick by brick, and of all the bad habits that suppress our natural abilities, worry would have to be one of the more pointless and destructive.

Worry serves no useful purpose. Unlike fear, which provokes a fight or flight response, or watchfulness, which prevents us stumbling into unseen dangers, worry is a paralysing emotion. Occasionally, it may do some good by serving as an alarm bell—worrying about whether or not you turned the iron off before you left the house might provoke a useful mental review of your pre-departure safety precautions. But having satisfactorily completed your procedures check-list (oven off, iron off, door locked, lamp-timer on to discourage burglars, cat de-sexed to discourage unwanted kittens, etc.) continuing to worry will do nothing positive. At best, it will force you to return home to discover either you did turn the iron off or your house is a smouldering ruin. Either way it's not going to change things.

## 65 Forgetting to change the things you can while worrying about the things you can't

For the ineffective, worry becomes a useful alibi for failing to act. Rather than addressing the issue, worrying about it becomes easier. If you have a problem with a colleague, far easier to sit and brood than engage in a constructive conversation to resolve it, or exact a puerile yet satisfying revenge by running a coin along his car. (Even then, the victory is short-lived; you immediately start worrying that you were caught on CCTV in the staff car park.) Worry also amplifies any problem. Take, for example, the crime rate. Despite a barrage of misinformation from the media and governments intent on law and order, crime rates have remained relatively stable for the last 150 years. Not many people know that. You're far more likely to be assaulted by a member of your family than by a stranger, which is comforting in an oddly marginal way. Likewise, walking to the shop poses a greater threat to your life than international terrorism, unless of course you're walking to a shop in Fallujiah.

## 66 Worrying about death by measles

## 67 Worrying about the threat of shark attack

## 68 Worrying about the decline in shark numbers

Make up your mind: either you like the sharks or you don't.

## 69 Feeling powerless in the face of everything that is wrong with the world

Firstly, remember what is right with the world. Shouldn't take long. Establish what is within your power to influence. You can't solve world poverty—it seems that no one can, not even Bono. But to alleviate your concern, you can begin to address your share of the culpability in the problem. For argument's sake, let's say $60 billion would go a fair way towards resolving the issue of food shortages in Africa. As one of 6 billion people in the world, donate $10. As one of the 1 billion people who can afford it, donate $60. (Remember that in 2006, the average citizen in the first world nation of Australia each spent more than $850 just on Christmas presents.)

Don't wait for someone else to go first; this is about improving your life as much as it is about that of anyone in the sub-Sahara. Ignore those who says it's a meaningless gesture—life is a meaningless gesture and whatever you do, no matter how small, to redress the imbalance of the world can only make you a better person. A word of caution: never get on the mailing list of a charity. They will badger you to the point where even Mother Theresa would rip up the next direct mail appeal.

Next, narrow your focus of concern. Rather than fretting about all the problems in the world, **actively concentrate on alleviating one**. Is it human rights, or land degradation, or whales, or the decline in public education? Choose a cause and champion it. Think locally—what can you do to improve the life of your neighbours, short of moving? Help out at your local senior citizens centre. Okay, the air's a bit stale and bingo gets tedious but you can add a bit of zing by shouting

'Bingo!' ninety seconds into the first game. At least you're doing something to help. Or visit an infirm relative and don't leave until they beg you to go.

I had a marvellous neighbour who died at the age of ninety-one, having lived in the same house since the age of three. He lived out his days on the pension but had about $20,000 in a savings account and, being a generous man, every year he divided the interest the money earned between his ten favourite charities. As far as I could tell, his only real concern in life was draining the rainwater out of his backyard; he worried quite a lot about guttering but he didn't let it completely ruin his day. There's a lesson in that for all of us.

## 70 Allowing fears of inadequate rainwater drainage to ruin your day

## 71 Worrying about strange lumps on your person

From a medical intervention point of view, there are two types of ineffective worriers. Those at the hypochondriacal end of the spectrum, who might as well live in the doctor's surgery; and those who refuse to see a doctor at all, preferring instead to surf the internet for a diagnosis of the nagging pain in the back where they think their kidneys are. If you have a physical problem that hasn't abated after two days in bed with a hot water bottle and some paracetamol, seek medical attention. Being told you're going to die is not going to alter the eventual outcome. It may even delay it.

## 72 Worrying about your superannuation

One of the less attractive aspects of increased life expectancy that no one really foresaw is that the increase comes at the end of life rather than more usefully at the beginning or in the middle. We're just painfully old for a lot longer. Gone are the comforting days of the fruitful working life then a short period of pottering about the shed before a cardio infarct carried us off in front of the tele. Having devolved themselves of any responsibility for their citizens, governments have thrown the financial onus for retirement back onto us, with the bizarre result that we now labour and fret to provide for a future we may not even reach. Like the Calvinists, we deny our present by investing too heavily in our as yet non-existent future. Always at the back of our minds is the nagging fear that there could be decades of getting by on the feeble amount of super we have spread over eight different funds, attracting nothing but administration fees.

Simple solution: don't worry about it. Put a bit aside into an industry fund each week and wait for something to turn up. By all means take heed of Aesop's fable of the industrious ant making hay while the sun shone but always remember to balance your inner ant with your inner grasshopper.

## 73 Worrying on behalf of other people

This is a beauty—did they ask you to? If worry does nothing for you, it does even less by proxy. Don't confuse worry for concern. Worried people observe from a futile distance; concerned people offer help.


Worry is only one of the many negative emotional states that plague the ineffective. There's also guilt, envy, vindictiveness, jealousy, anger, unsubstantiated fear and existential nausea, to name but a few. Space and innate apathy forbid an exhaustive review of all the emotional cul-de-sacs you'll walk into but here's a random selection to chew over …

## 74  Thinking guilt is the end, not the means

Legitimate guilt can be a useful thing. It can prevent us from pursuing a wrongful course of action or, if we have transgressed, guilt can provoke remorse and an act of contrition. Sadly, too often guilt marks the end of it, almost as if the emotional discomfort we feel is considered adequate punishment and any actual atonement is unnecessary. Sorry, but just feeling guilty is not enough.

And our ability to recognise when we need to make amends has been compromised by this age of litigation in which the simple act of saying sorry is seen as an admission of wrongdoing. And, more importantly, possible financial culpability. We are increasingly incapable of admitting fault and equally incapable of apology—even graciously accepting apologies is becoming more problematic. So if you've done something you know to be wrong, make amends.

## 75  Refusing to concede fault

## 76  Not being able to say you're sorry

## 77  Not being able to accept an apology—and mean it

## 78  Feeling guilty when you've done nothing wrong

As a tool of social control, guilt is brilliant—even more so when we are made to feel guilty when we haven't actually done anything wrong! Recognise what is a legitimate transgression and your degree of culpability. What constitutes a sin in your moral code? Maybe what others regard as a guilty secret is perfectly acceptable behaviour within your own personal value system. (Try to temper your personal value system with some sort of ethics—the Yorkshire Ripper had a personal value system but it's not one you'd happily recommend.) Are you feeling guilty because you didn't intervene to stop someone else's wrongdoing? Their actions are not your responsibility. Are you feeling guilty because you've broken your New Year's resolutions? It's not a crime—find some other word to describe the feelings provoked by your inability to keep your resolve, like disappointed, resigned, rueful, abashed, or fat bastard who will still look like the side of a barn in six months' time.

## 79 Doing things because you feel you should, rather than because you want to

More often than not, we feel guilty if we fail to discharge some sort of obligational duty, like sending thank you cards or remembering a birthday. This is not genuine guilt; this is fear of being judged for not doing something that you didn't really want to do in the first place. Feel selfish and thankless by all means but not guilty. If you genuinely want to send thank you cards you will; to do so under duress rather misses the point. Don't say 'I feel guilty about not ringing Aunty Pip on her birthday'—either get on the phone or forget it. Don't use perceived guilt as an excuse for inaction. Obviously there are unwanted duties which must be done and it's hard to find the joy in everything. But don't let it become a pattern; jihadists aside, the martyr complex may be attractive to some people but it's rarely life-enhancing.

## 80  Believing in God because you feel you should rather than because you need to

Religion is the home of organised guilt, being as it is the home of sin. One of the by-products of today's secularised society has been a resurgence in religious or spiritual belief. Sensing a hollowness at the core of existence, many are tempted to fill it with belief in a higher being, ignoring (if I may say as I head out along a limb) all evidence to the contrary. Every other animal resists the temptation to build temples, giving us humans the dubious distinction of being the only rational beings who behave irrationally. But if you insist on ignoring the Age of Enlightenment and the relentless march of scientific knowledge and join some band of God botherers who gather in convention centres on light industrial estates, ask yourself this: when you transgress the moral code of whatever church you belong to are you genuinely remorseful or just worried that you'll be found out and punished? Is it the fear of retribution, divine or otherwise, that drives your anxiety or an honest need for repentance? If you've sinned against God, is your repentance going to make Him feel better or you?

And one other thing—if you do feel a need to have personal religious beliefs, remember they are just that: personal. No need to spread the word.

## 81  Falling victim to the politics of envy

This is happening everywhere: at a national level, in the workplace, the schoolyard, the family—even in the gym, where they have those floor-to-ceiling mirrors and everybody looks more cut than you do. Envy is one of the major drivers of consumerism, that old 'keeping up with the Joneses' mentality that has served marketers so well for so long. You'd think we'd be wise to it by now! Along with fear, envy is fast becoming the favourite strategic tool of governments as they play off one interest group against another, calculating just how many wedges need to be driven into the electorate to guarantee a majority result at the ballot box.

Again, like so many other aspects of the feeling of ineffectiveness, envy is motivated by a lack of self-belief, a lack of personal fulfilment. The American writer Gore Vidal said with painful honesty: 'Whenever a friend succeeds, a little something in me dies.' And that's his friends he's talking about! Hard as it may be, try to revel in another's achievements. Success need not be a finite prize pool that can only be apportioned to the few—to the optimistic relativist, success can be anything you make it to be. If you're a loser, congratulate the winners with good grace because without you they'd be nothing.

## 82   Holding grudges

A complete waste of time that does you more damage than anyone else. Feuds, vendettas and revenge demean all concerned. It takes two to take offence—by allowing yourself to be offended, you are immediately complicit in negativity. Rise above it. If you believe the grievance is genuine, resolve it quickly; even if the result is not everything you hoped for, you've made an effort and are the moral superior of your opponent. And that is the sweetest revenge of all.

## 83   Forgetting forgiveness does more for you than for the forgiven

## 84　Confusing solitude with loneliness

Loneliness, the unpleasant by-product of vigorous individualism, is a horrible thing. Solitude, on the other hand, can be wonderful. The lonely have little choice but to be so; solitude is a voluntary condition. A respite from the noise and agitation of modern life, moments of quiet introspection allow you to reflect on just how badly your life is going.

## 85　Confusing sadness with depression

Depression—and more significantly the chemical treatment of it—are on the rise in western societies. For the pharmaceutical companies, every black cloud has a silver lining. It's an awkward truism that depression is something better avoided than treated but, in the pursuit of happiness, don't be afraid of moments of sadness; they're a natural part of life. Even bi-polar has its upside. In fact, long before the invention of Prozac, mournful ennui was known more positively as melancholia and regarded as something that could be usefully embraced to experience a complete emotional life. The romantic poets couldn't get enough of it—wandering wistfully along an autumnal stream and gazing lugubriously at the odd drooping flower led to all sorts of acts of creativity. Embrace misery when it visits you—but don't forget to firmly bid it farewell when it has outlived its usefulness.

## 86　Lacking the creative imagination of the romantic poets

# 9
# WELL, IF THAT'S WHAT YOU THINK OF ME

'Honest criticism is hard to take, particularly from a relative, a friend, an acquaintance, or a stranger.'
*Franklin P Jones*

This page is for note-taking. As if.

One thing the ineffective person is well acquainted with is criticism. They can smell a patronising remark from 200 metres upwind. It doesn't even have to be real; offence can be taken without any provocation. No one is more thin-skinned than the ineffective; if they were a duck's back, they'd drown. Taking criticism is tough for even the most secure of us—you have every right to say what you want but I'll fight to the death for my right to disagree with it! But the acknowledgement of legitimate criticism is an important lesson that we all must learn. Sadly, few of us do.

Equally important is the ability to openly and methodically refute unwarranted criticism. Determining what is fair criticism is a skill that requires self-honesty—a tricky proposition at the best of times, and one often beyond someone who can stare in a mirror and convince themselves they look ten years younger by breathing in. (Here's a tip to disabuse yourself of that particular conceit: look in the mirror then tilt your head over sideways until it's parallel with the ground. Behold the humbling effects of gravity as your face drops eagerly towards your shoulder.)

## 87  Thinking breathing in makes you look younger

## 88  Going into a depressive spiral when you tilt your head sideways in a mirror

## 89  Being unable to honestly appraise your abilities

Before you can be good at something, you have to find what you're good at. Before you can effectively take constructive criticism, you need to develop a sense of your own self-worth—to recognise value not in what you'd like yourself to be but in what you are. There is nothing intrinsically wrong with aspiration but it can cloud self-judgement. Have you ever said: 'I could do that, if only:

- ❖ I worked harder
- ❖ I had more time
- ❖ I had more money
- ❖ I lost five kilos
- ❖ people recognised my talents
- ❖ others gave me respect
- ❖ I could be bothered.'

Doubtless it's sometimes true. But aspiration can become a state of self-denial. Far better to recognise what you can do **now** rather than at some unspecified time in the future.

## 90  Being afraid to admit ignorance

## 91 Being unwilling to learn

Pride in achievement is admirable; pride that prevents discovery is not. Never be afraid to admit you don't know how to do something. Don't be afraid to read the instruction manual. (That is if you can make head or tail of it.) Too often the ineffective, to save face or avoid looking foolish, refuse to acknowledge their inability to complete a task. Ask for help. When someone shows you how to do something, you not only acquire new skills but also realise that they've usually gone and done what needed doing in the first place. Saves you the bother.

## 92 Only respecting the opinions of those who agree with you

## 93 Fearing the arbitrary judgement of others

Learn to determine whose opinions you respect, not just the opinions of people who agree with you. Equally, listen to the judgements of those you don't value so highly and understand exactly why you can afford to ignore them. Sometimes even those you don't respect can say truthful things. But, as a rule, work towards the approval of people you admire without making the mistake of relying on it.

Ideally, the good opinion of others should simply serve as an affirmation of what you inwardly know you have already achieved in your own right.

Fearing judgement will prevent you from action. Never forget that we are all essentially alike—those who sit in judgement are equally fearful of being judged themselves. Simply present the work and let it be judged on its own merits by people whose opinions you respect. And if even then they don't like it, fuck 'em.

## 94 Assuming that everyone automatically wants you to fail

If you have to make a presentation or apply for a job, don't immediately assume that your audience or selection panel are looking for you to fail. As a matter of fact, they want to give you the job—otherwise they wouldn't be seeing you. They may not, for any number of reasons, be able to give you the job or accept your pitch, but it's not because they didn't want to from the outset. As an actor, I've been for any number of auditions and failed in most of them. It took me a long time to realise that it was nothing personal; the producers or directors had asked to see me because they thought I was potentially right for the part—they were willing me to succeed and were equally disappointed that I was too tall, too short, wore glasses or couldn't act my way out of a wet paper bag.

## 95 Seeing criticism where none was intended

## 96 Accepting criticism that you know to be unfounded

If you know the work is good, don't cop unfair criticism. Usually we allow it because we're fearful of losing the job, offending a potential employer or want to avoid conflict in a personal relationship. Not refuting unwarranted criticism can only lead to resentment. Argue the case for what you have done—throw the onus back on them to justify their opinions. You'd be surprised at how quickly they'll reappraise their opinions or ask you to pack your desk and leave quietly before security arrives.

# 10

# PUTTING IT TOGETHER: ORGANISE!

'First comes thought; then organisation of that thought, into ideas and plans; then transformation of those plans into reality. The beginning, as you will observe, is in your imagination.'
*Napoleon Hill (1883–1970)*

This page allocated for idle doodling only!

And for most of us, the end is in your imagination as well. I mean, it's all very well for people like Napoleon Hill, born in a two-room cabin in rural Virginia. Have you ever heard of a self-made man who *wasn't* born in a two-room cabin? Despite his humble beginnings, and his mother permanently leaving the two-room cabin for a better life with Jesus when he was only ten, Hill went on to become an industrious leech who latched onto Andrew Carnegie, one of the richest men in the world, and was commissioned by the tycoon to find out what made the most successful people of the time tick. He wrote up his series of interviews (unpaid, which gives you an idea of how Andrew Carnegie got so rich) into the self-help bestseller *Think and Grow Rich*. Like it's that easy! Voltaire, Bertrand Russell or Thomas Aquinas made a fortune out of thinking? I think not.

But there is a key observation Hill makes in his pithy little PowerPoint presentation slide: organisation. Most highly ineffective people remain that way because they can't get organised. Their lives are lived in a permanent state of chaos, lurching from one badly planned crisis to the next ill-conceived disaster. Their desks are covered in mounds of unpaid bills and un-filed correspondence, their wardrobes are a clutter of badly folded shirts and odd socks and their sheds are piled to the roof with crap that they think might come in handy one day. Believe me: it never will. If you haven't used something within two years, get rid of it. Unless it's a Zimmer frame. Slowly sinking beneath a growing mountain of things-to-do, the highly ineffective lose sight of how to turn it all around, to clear a work surface so they can make a start in a rational, effective way.

A growth industry has sprung up to cater for the angst of the badly organised. Franchise retail outlets selling storage solutions, books and websites offering organisational tips for everything from tidying cables to streamlining personal finances—even bill-paying services that bundle all your household accounts into one monthly invoice that you can get around to paying eventually if only you can find the bloody thing. But many people don't even recognise the problem. On a website dedicated to the sharing of personal goals in the hope of inspiring others, the subject 'Actively work on my organisational skills' attracted only one person who thought the goal was worthwhile. Are you guilty of:

**97 Saying 'If I tidy this up, I won't know where anything is!'**

**98 Thinking a budget is just a matter of keeping your receipts**

**99 Buying two trays of asparagus for the price of one when you live alone**

## 100 Paying off credit cards with other credit cards

If you said yes to just one of the above, you either love asparagus or have a lack of organisational skills that will impact every aspect of your life.

## 101 Making nouns into verbs

## 102 Being a pedantic git

So let's break down this chapter into some manageable subsets, then categorise each in an ascending order of importance and explore some alphabetised options for immediate, mid- and long-term solutions. Let's look at:

- ❖ Personal Finance
- ❖ In the Home Office
- ❖ Project Management on Urban Infrastructure.

Now you might think that last one is going too far but what if you're suddenly asked to implement a major refurbishment of culverts and stormwater management systems in your local area? Learn to expect—and plan for—the unexpected.

## PERSONAL FINANCE

The amount of advice offered today on how to handle your money (should you be lucky enough to have any) is mind-boggling. The daily papers now run a personal money management section every week. Is there anything about money that changes in a week? These columns are as much use as the financial reports on television news bulletins, spending a minute at most telling us that the oil/gold/stock market index price has gone up or down. I'm no financial planner but I suspect that's a little short of the detail we need to make informed investment decisions.

There has been an exponential growth in the number of financial service products available, most beyond the understanding of mere mortals and requiring an army of planners, accountants and advisers to make sense of it. All at a cost, of course. With governments moving away from social benefits for the ageing population and relying more heavily on superannuation, the fear of not having enough to live on in retirement is infecting us all. As if you didn't have enough to worry about while you're working; the thought of an extended old age where you can't afford to go out your front door more than once a year is enough to turn your hair grey. Or greyer. But is there any subject in the world more boring than superannuation?

### 103 Banging on about superannuation plans

### 104 Having no superannuation plan

More of that later. Like so many aspects of modern life, the volume of advice over what you should do with your money threatens to paralyse any decision making. It all becomes too much to deal with; at the mere mention of indexed growth I want to retire to a dark room with a cold flannel. So let's keep it simple.

### 105 Having no household budget strategy

This is the most common bad habit of the financially disorganised. Time was when strategy was something that only generals and chess geeks need worry about. Now, sadly, every

## Putting It Together: Organise!

aspect of our lives seems to require strategic thinking. Even driving the car to work needs to be meticulously planned by taking into account weather conditions, traffic reports, known or suspected road works, adequacy of fuel supply (yes, you should have filled up yesterday instead of hoping for an overnight drop in world oil prices) and remembering where you actually parked the car. (Not so strange—I have a friend who dropped his car off to the mechanic in the morning through the haze of an extreme hang-over. At the end of the day, noticing that his all but worthless car was not outside his house, he assumed it was stolen and couldn't be bothered reporting it to the police. He was somewhat surprised when the mechanic rang eight months later to ask if he was ever going to pick his car up. Started first time, too.)

But I digress. Here's a handy budgeting tip I picked up from somewhere: go into a two-dollar shop and buy a notebook. Write down everything you spend—everything—and you'll soon realise just how much money you waste. And the biggest waste of money has been the two dollars you spent on the notebook because after a week you can't bear to look at it.

That's just one of the many home budgeting strategies available, all suggesting that you write a detailed list of weekly expenditure and attempt to reconcile it to your available income. A largely pointless exercise for the ineffective, who haven't moved beyond the following short list.

1.    Make household budget strategy.

But by listing all your bills and expenses, you not only have a good idea of where your money goes but you can also identify savings. A typical 'budget trimming' program looks like this:

| Item | Cost | Weekly Saving | Annual Saving |
|---|---|---|---|
| Daily cappuccino | $2.50 | $17.50 | $910.00 |
| Bought lunch | $9.50 | $66.50 | $3458.00 |
| Dining out | $49.00 | $98.00 | $5096.00 |
| Bottle of wine | $18.00 | $126.00 | $6552.00 |
| Theatre tickets | $75.00 |  | $37.50 (amortised) |
| DVD hire | $8.00 | $32.00 | $1664.00 |
| Massage | $90.00 | $90.00 | $4680.00 |

Even cutting out those simple 'extras' saves you a whopping $22,397.50 a year! With a little extra effort and some serious belt-tightening, many people can potentially save more than they earn. Isn't the financial system amazing?

Think of ways you can reduce your conspicuous consumption. Make a checklist of things you could do without—do you really need that gym membership? Why not select a gym a brisk half-hour's walk away from home? Simply walk to the gym, turn round and go back—all the exercise you need. To emulate that 'just been to the gym' experience, don't wear deodorant. Could you do without your mobile phone? Hannibal managed to cross the Alps and bring the Roman Empire almost to its knees without one—maybe you could too. Don't buy just one bottle of wine from the bottle shop; they're far cheaper by the dozen and then there's always one handy in the fridge for when you decide to kick on.

It was a character of Charles Dickens, the indefatigable Mr Micawber, who, despite spending much of his time in debtors' prison and having the commercial acumen of a hamster, gave the most basic and sound financial advice ever uttered: 'Annual income twenty pounds, annual expenditure nineteen pounds nineteen and six, result happiness. Annual income twenty pounds, annual expenditure twenty pounds ought and six, result misery.'

Of course that was in the days before futures options or hedged funds and a financial planner would argue that if Micawber had put ten pounds onto the short-term money market he could have made some serious cash, but the simple common sense of **spend less money than you earn** is a sound financial lesson for all of us.

How simple is that?

SPEND LESS MONEY THAN YOU EARN.

But bad news for the highly ineffective: we live in a credit society and levels of household debt have never been higher. Apparently, it's now in the national interest to spend more money than you earn. In 2006, Australian consumer debt topped $37 billion, which averaged out at $2811 per household, not counting mortgages—and that's just on the plastic. Still, that figure is a mere drop in the bucket compared to the USA, where consumer debt hit $2.2 *trillion* in 2005. Three out of five American families were paying an average of $1700 a year in late fees and interest charges on their credit cards alone. Many card-holders were reduced to making minimum payments. It's been calculated that, on a $3000 credit balance at a 17.5 per cent annual interest rate, paying only the minimum payment (calculated at a 1.5 per cent minimum payment rate) will take *95 years* to clear the debt.

## 106 Not paying the full amount owing on a credit card statement

Of course, the whole point of credit cards is to encourage you to spend beyond your ability to pay them off in full each time the statement arrives. Credit providers efficiently make profits because their customers are generally inefficient. Some people manage to clear the debt in one transaction but the credit providers make the lion's share of their profits from those who can't. And these are hungry lions.

Credit cards also create debt that is not leveraged against assets—a mortgage entails a higher level of indebtedness but unless you made a terrible mistake in timing your entry into the housing market, you have the house as collateral. However, I think we can safely say that the modular lounge and fokari rug you bought as an impulse purchase on Mastercard will probably not retain their value; nearly everything bought on credit cards is to be consumed (travel, accommodation, vodka, etc.), has already been consumed (groceries, utility bills, brothel visits and so on) or has halved in value within twenty-four hours of purchase (modular lounge, fokari rug). Possible exceptions are rare Picassos or collectable early twentieth-century ceramics—got any of those hanging around? Didn't think so.

## 107 Switching to another credit card

Otherwise known as changing horses midstream. There are any number of cards on offer that lure you with the promise of low or no-interest honeymoon periods if you roll over your existing debt. Looks like a good idea but, as with any honeymoon, you can pretty well guarantee you'll get screwed.

Credit providers aren't doing this because they feel sorry for you; in an increasingly crowded market, they're hunting for suckers like you who pay over and over again for things they didn't need in the first place. Look closely at any offer—what are the hidden fees and charges? What happens when the honeymoon is over? Or are you just attracted to the offer because you can choose the colour of your card or put a photo of your choice on it? How cool is that?

Sorry, the only personal statement a credit card makes is 'I'm an idiot.'

Even so, to many people the offer of consolidating a variety of debts into one can be attractive. Yes, you will reduce the numbers of service fees you pay and the low interest period can save you money if you **pay off the entire amount**. But you're still not tackling the central problem: you spend too much, stupid!

### 108  Using multiple credit cards

See all of above but with bells on.

### 109  Increasing the limit on your credit card whenever the bank suggests it

Some of you may remember the quaint old-fashioned practice of having to practically beg a bank to lend you money. What naïve, innocent times! After crawling in to the bank manager's office on your hands and knees and offering your first-born as security, you might have been grudgingly given a loan with all the grace of Shylock after he lost the court case. But today a bank service representative (or customer liaison operative— the smiles are free!) will offer you money in the comfort of your own home or even over the phone—they'd probably quite happily throw it at you from a passing car. And because we're obliged under threat of prosecution to repay any money we borrow, and our fear of taking a shower in prison is up there with being buried alive, they know they'll get it back eventually. With interest.

It's an illusory offer, more money to pay off the money you already owe. Casinos thrive on it. By offering you a higher credit card limit, the bank takes a minimal risk. They know if you **can** spend more money, you **will**.

The other psychological trap of credit cards is our inability to keep track of what we've spent on them. Paying in cash gives you an immediate sense of your financial position—when it's gone, it's gone. Credit, on the other hand, is illusory. How many times have you looked at a card statement and struggled to remember when or why you made that purchase? Plastic money was created for the impulse buyer. Whereas cash shopping entails the effort of withdrawing the money, noting the available balance and safeguarding the wad, buying with a credit card requires no more thought than remembering to bring it.

## 110 Making purchases on credit for no apparent reason

## 111 Buying on credit for the frequent flier points

## 112 Thinking Ikea furniture will be tomorrow's antiques

Tricky one, because I think some of those bedside tables made with real wood could be worth a lot one day. Certain pieces in the streamlined Nordic-look might just be the next Chippendale. Like in a thousand years. But if you insist, make sure you store it well and avoid using Mr Sheen on the varnished surfaces. What am I saying? You're ineffective—as if you'd clean!

### 113 Buying something just because it's a bargain

How many times have you heard this? 'I had to get it because it was so cheap!' Well, yes, I'm sure it was but why does anyone need a bean bag with inbuilt stereo and massage pads? And more to the point, why does anyone need two?

### 114 Living on eBay

eBay addiction is far worse than trawling the net for porn because it costs more and it takes a lot longer. Like all aspects of modern consumerism it's largely driven by want, not need, and potentially combines all the psychological traps discussed thus far. Add the risk of online fraud and it's a recipe for financial disaster. To use eBay successfully requires **discipline** and if you've learnt anything so far (and that's a big if) it's that ineffective people and discipline rarely occur in the same sentence.

Even if you can conquer your addiction to credit cards, there are many other ways you can kiss your money goodbye. Figures show an alarming surge in the popularity of the redraw facility or line-of-credit mortgages. Danger Will Robinson! This is money on the never-never that Peter Pan could only dream of.

### 115 Forgetting that banks are smarter and craftier than you are

## 116 Using mortgage lines of credit inadvisably

In a housing market where many mortgagees are struggling to pay even the interest component of a loan, extending your principal borrowings can border on the financially suicidal. In some low-doc, or no-doc, loans, usually negotiated with people who've been knocked back by larger credit providers, the loan-to-value ratio is a huge 105 per cent, a ratio that can only increase as housing prices deflate in a cooling market.

Equally dangerous is the inter-generational housing loan. House prices being astronomically high and the notion of home ownership being so firmly entrenched in the modern psyche, mortgage providers are now offering loans that extend beyond your working lifetime—fifty- or sixty-year mortgages that your children will inherit. The interest paid on loans of that repayment length can be almost triple the amount borrowed. Here's an example:

$350,000 at 7% over 25 years: interest paid $392,119
$350,000 at 7% over 40 years: interest paid $694,000

And even worse, you pay off a mortgage for your whole life without ever knowing that sweet moment, that once-in-a-lifetime opportunity to go into a bank with the final payment and say 'Stick this up your arse!' before you realise that you were actually also there to apply for a personal loan to cover your outstanding credit card debts.

## 117 Bad timing of moments of hollow triumphalism

Who really benefits from increasing your debt? Even in a small economy like Australia's, in 2006 the five major banks had combined a profit of more than $16 billion—$800 for every man, woman and child in the country. Banks benefit. And the long period of low interest rates that the world has enjoyed for the past ten years or so will come to an end. If history tells us anything it's that good times don't last. But in the Great Depression (and still no one knows what was so great about it) levels of personal indebtedness were much lower. Home ownership rates were lower. Next time Wall Street crashes through the floor, we've all got a lot more to lose. How exposed are you to debt?

There is another hidden cost to debt-driven consumerism. How can you begin to quantify the stress and anxiety that it brings to people's lives? Well, to borrow from the Mastercard advertising campaign: it's priceless. Think about why you're going down this path. Is it to satisfy some short-term material desire, whether for a new bathroom, an overseas trip or extensive cosmetic surgery? (Probably not a bad idea in some cases—if you're going broke, you might as well look good.) Will it make you feel better? An increasing number of studies show that the return of happiness or positive feelings on spending actually decreases the more frequently you spend. A new computer can make you feel good for a few days; a new car might bring positive emotions for only a few weeks. The anxiety of paying for it all will last for years.

### 118 Buying to make yourself feel better

### 119 Buying to make yourself feel more important

The psychology of consumerism, of buying beyond your actual physical needs, is a fascinating area. Do we buy because we're unhappy or are we unhappy because we buy? Studies have shown that **non-materialists** (people who feel no pressing need to own material goods) register the greatest level of happiness. Once they've bought a tambourine and a bible, they're pretty much set. **Rich materialists** who can afford to buy whatever they desire almost catch up in the happiness stakes, but **poor materialists**, lacking the means to finance their wants, are the unhappiest sods of all. No prizes for guessing which category the ineffective fall into!

## 120 Being a poor materialist

Tim Kasser, in his book *The High Price of Materialism*, found that when people organise their lives around extrinsic goals such as the acquisition of material goods, they report greater unhappiness in relationships, poorer moods and more psychological problems. Compounding this unhappiness is the increasing paralysis we modern consumers feel in the face of the rampant availability of choice. As we have seen in Chapter 5, the Decisional Procrastinator avoids making decisions by endlessly researching alternatives. The same applies to consumers; author Barry Schwartz, in his book *The Paradox of Choice*, labels this type of shopper the 'maximizer', forever comparing deals and models, perhaps saving money as a result but ultimately less happy, always harbouring doubt that maybe there was a better option just around the corner. To delineate the other type, Schwartz borrows from 1978 Nobel Laureate Herbert Simon, who coined the term *satisficer*—the type that believes the merely excellent will do, as opposed to the absolute best. The wider the range of choice available, the harder it is to be a satisficer.

Tests have proven the hypothesis. Shoppers who were offered free samples of a range of six jams were more likely to make a purchase than those who were offered a choice of twenty-four. Schwartz cites the example of his local hi-fi store. On sale were 74 different stereo tuners, 55 CD players, 32 tape players and 50 sets of speakers. Combined in an average sound system, they offered 6,512,00 permutations! Faced with such a staggering array, the average maximizer flees the store and ends up a quivering heap in the local Starbucks trying to choose between twenty blends, five types of milk and three levels of froth. Meanwhile, the satisficer buys a three-in-one. Or a radio.

### 121 Not being satisfied with being a satisficer

Before you head out on a shopping trip, ask yourself this: why are so many people intent on making me buy something? Obviously, the manufacture and exchange of goods helps the economy function—someone's got to keep all those Chinese people employed at a dollar a week. But the consumerist economy is a false one, based as it is on the spurious notion of perpetual economic growth. To fuel that growth, you must buy things that you **want** rather than **need** and it requires legions of workers constantly prodding you to get out there and spend, to keep you on the 'hedonic treadmill'—advertisers, marketers, sales analysts, psychologists, developers and those ghastly spruikers who stand outside discount variety shops bellowing at you to take a look inside.

### 122 Taking the advice of a spruiker and having a look inside

### 123 Exiting the store with a purchase

Even the staples of human existence have been subsumed into this voracious corporate maw. Food, once a fairly rudimentary basic requirement, would now be all but unrecognisable to our hunter–gatherer ancestors. (So would we—they were three feet tall, hairy and smelled like washing left in the machine overnight.) The typical first-world supermarket stocks 30,000 items. Every year, 20,000 new lines are trialled. Most fail spectacularly but others succeed, adding another five varieties of unsalted lo-fat peanut butter to the shelves, or another ten brands of bottled drinking water.

## 124 Drinking bottled water

Clean drinking water from a tap was one of the great technological and medical advances of the industrial revolution. (The Romans also had the idea but made the mistake of making their pipes out of lead. Eventually, you could never get a plumber in Rome—they'd all died of lead poisoning.) But now tap water is no longer good enough. Not only must you now carry water with you wherever you go—because God knows you can die of thirst within half-an-hour—but it must be bottled from a mineral spring, which in the water business is a French word for tap. Bottled water is marketing's greatest triumph. We flush our toilets with water of a purity that would have the developing world panting and yet we feel a pressing need to drink bottled water. As the planet burns and global warming promises to see us all off, we happily bottle, process and truck water all over the country then pay more for it than petrol or beer, while all the time there's a perfectly adequate supply piped to within walking distance.

The most effective way to control your spending of money is to simply ask: 'Why am I doing this?' You'll be surprised at how many times you stop yourself and go and buy a bottle of champagne instead to celebrate your newfound resolve.

Next question is: I've stopped spending it, so how do I save it? If the financial system has invented a myriad of ways to relieve you of your money, it's also doing a fair job at preventing the unwary from saving it. Like with so many aspects of modern living, eternal vigilance is required.

## 125 Having more than one bank account

The highly ineffective have accounts everywhere—mortgage with one bank, personal loan with another, income deposits in another and a Christmas Club savings account with a balance of $18.32 somewhere else. All attracting fees, all generating statements to add to the growing pile in the drawer.

While we're on the subject of drawers, a cautionary tale. A friend of mine has a drawer in which he puts little projects that he has to get around to—repairing a clock, cleaning corrosion off the emergency torch because he hasn't changed the batteries since the power crisis of the 1970s, filling in the guarantee on his Walkman, that sort of thing. He calls this Gepetto's drawer, after the puppeteer who whittled life into Pinocchio. It's a rainy day drawer, a tinkering drawer. Only trouble is, it's now a drawer the size of a garage. If he could squeeze the dishwasher that broke down two years ago into it, he would. Remember: if something goes into a drawer, eventually it's got to come out.

## 126 Not emptying the Gepetto drawer

The easiest thing to do with multiple bank accounts is to consolidate and simplify. By all means, take a little time to compare the banks but don't spend too long on this—the margins are fractional and life is way too short. Don't chop and change: many fees and nearly all of the frustrating problems associated with any of life's transactions occur in the setup. This applies across the board—switching telephone companies, internet providers or utilities invariably attracts a host of problems that quickly outweigh any potential advantage. If you're onto a remotely good thing, stick to it.

Having found a local bank you like, open one account with a phone banking facility. Cut up all but one of your credit cards, particularly those offered by department stores. But the important thing here is: use the credit card only for purchases that *cannot be made in any other way*, like car rental. If you can pay cash for it, do not use the credit card.

Organise for your salary to be paid directly into the account and set up direct debit for all your regular bills and mortgage or rent payments. (But don't forget that British banks reportedly collected £500 million in forgotten un-cancelled direct debits in 2005.) If the bank offers motor, home and contents insurance and you feel you need it, take it and have it directly transferred from your account. Allow yourself one cash withdrawal per week and live on that: no exceptions. Monitor the system for a few months to make sure it all works, ensuring that all direct debits are synchronised and operating. Then leave it and **never think about it again**.

## 127 Chopping and changing financial strategies

Financial advisers on talkback radio will tell you to open a mortgage maximiser account, a checking account for daily expenses, a term deposit online for savings that offers a high rate yet flexible access to your money, blah blah blah. That's because they find this stuff interesting—no one else does. It's all you can do to handle a passbook. For most of us, the financial equation is simple: not much money comes in, all of it goes out. Anything else is mere tinkering round the edges.

It's hard to resist the pressure of the constant options being thrown at you but ultimately the options are not there for your benefit. They are ways to increase someone else's prosperity, not yours. We fall victim to the sales pitch because we live in constant fear that we're missing out on something, that off-peak electricity might be 0.052 cents a megawatt cheaper with that other power company and if we switch now we could be richer. Yes—you could buy an orange with the annual saving. Don't switch—sit in the dark for one hour a week and you'll save exactly the same amount.

## 128 Trading in shares

We're all shareholders now, of course, with our superannuation and the few modest stocks we were given when everything in public ownership was privatised. We were even offered the choice to buy more of what we once owned, which was nice of them. This curious trend of forcing the public to buy what it created stems back to the dry economic policies of Thatcher and Reagan, when the world turned against the social-democratic liberalism of the post-war period and the cult of the individual was reinstated to champion the causes of globalisation and the deregulation of the financial sector. Not surprisingly, the promised trickle-down effect of economic benefit defied gravity and largely trickled up, with the richest people in the world becoming vastly richer while a few crumbs were scattered about to keep the rest of us happily delusional.

We became known as the mums-and-dads investors (which is the economic term for feeble amateur), the hope being that the returns on our pathetic stakes would discourage us from questioning corporate decisions. As long as our dividends and share prices stayed healthy, we wouldn't rock the boat. It seems to have worked. CEO salaries have risen astronomically in the past two decades. In 1982, the average US CEO earned forty-two times as much as the average non-management worker. By 2004, that ratio had risen to 431:1. Can one person be worth more than 431 times that of the average worker in an enterprise? No is the answer you're looking for.

Share trading is not rocket science—it's share trading. There was a famous Swedish experiment in the 1960s that compared the share trading expertise of a stockbroker (remember them?), an accountant and a monkey. Each was given an amount of money to invest to see how much profit they could make. The monkey selected its stocks by throwing darts at a list of the companies trading on the stock exchange. Through sheer chance, it hit a mineral exploration company that went through the roof on a speculative bubble the next day. The monkey cleaned up—the accountant made a modest gain and the stockbroker went backwards.

What does this prove? Not a lot, but it does indicate that quick gains on the stock market are akin to a lottery. Online trading has bred a generation of penny-stock traders addicted to the speculative volatility of the market. It's not unlike playing poker for one-cent pieces—mildly amusing for a time but after a while it becomes as tedious as watching golf.

Don't attempt it yourself. The stock market is no place for those who think risk management is carrying a change of underwear. If you feel a pressing need to be exposed to the world of international finance, transfer some money to an ethical investment portfolio, knowing that your money isn't financing land degradation, depleted uranium warheads or the film career of Rob Schneider.

## 129 Forgetting the golden rule: keep it simple

# 11
# LET'S GET PERSONAL

'Man is the only animal that blushes. Or needs to.'
*Mark Twain*

This page has the chapter heading on the reverse side. If you're reading this first, you're reading the book backwards.

Man is a social animal. No other beast in creation organises cocktail parties, Thai banquets or Human Resources Departments. Admittedly, the higher primates form complicated social structures but rarely does a gibbon sit and brood about not fitting in. Ineffective humans, on the other hand, fret and fume as they stumble through the intricate web of social interaction, believing that their lives will be made or broken as they desperately try to decipher the signals and behavioural codes of the people around them. And they've got a point; nothing can kill a career faster than an ill-timed *faux pas* at the CEO's meet-and-greet wine and cheese night.

Here are a few of the social obstacles thrown up along the course of the human race ...

## 130 Being boring

All of us live in fear of being thought of as dull. Is there anything worse than when, mid-conversation, you register the eyes of the other person drifting off to look at an intriguing brick wall in preference to you? Some people try to make themselves more interesting; memorising jokes, attending Toastmasters for confidence in public speaking or becoming the unofficial source of office gossip. Others struggle on bravely, boring the limbs of their colleagues rigid at corporate functions, until there's no one left to talk to except the waiters, who are under a professional obligation to listen.

Here's a tip for the conversationally challenged. Talk about the other person: make every thing you say a question about their life. You'd be surprised how happy people are to talk endlessly about themselves. The conversation may become somewhat stilted if you both try the same tactic, so should your fellow converser be equally dull, enjoy a companionable silence instead.

Or expand your interests. Don't despair if you have no natural talents that make you entertaining company. Enrol in an adult education course on a fascinating but little known subject. You'll find the class full of equally boring people who'll make you look good.

## 131 Being overly enthusiastic

The relentlessly jolly or the hearty sporting type with a crushing handshake are best avoided, as is anyone 'high on life'. Devout Christians often have an inner glow that serves as a warning beacon to steer clear. Don't try too hard to be keen; a sense of reserve can be intriguing, but don't retire to the point of invisibility. The keynote is balance: modest yet confident, informed but never a know-it-all, amusing but not Phyllis Diller.

## 132 Trying to be funny every waking hour

Until the advent of online pornography (see below) stand-up comedy was briefly considered to be the new rock and roll. In the non-professional world, many ineffective people have taken this as a green light and feel a pressing need to be funny, despite all evidence to the contrary. We all have a sense of humour but few of us can be funny, just as we can all brush our teeth but few are licensed to practise dentistry. Modern television comedy has tried to help as much as possible, reducing an entire series to one or two catch-phrases that can be memorised by even the slowest; but anyone who can say 'I'm the only gay in the village!' ten times a day is just as unfunny as an older colleague who can recite the entire script of *Monty Python and the Holy Grail*. Unless naturally gifted, leave the comedy stylings for close friends and family—they've always known there's something funny about you.

## 133 Being shy

There is a big difference between modesty and shyness. Shyness is a habit that should be broken; modesty is a virtue that should be sought. Too often the painfully shy cut themselves off from life by wearing their shyness as some sort of perverse badge of honour. Instilled by parents with an unhealthy suspicion of the extroverted, shyness ultimately achieves nothing. By all means be retiring, but keep your shyness well hidden in a darkened room.

## 134 Using another's anecdote as a springboard for your own

The ineffective will often try to raise the conversational ante. When told of a holiday, they'll have been there as well but for half the price; if someone's been ill, they've had the same virus but much worse. The writer Alan Bennett quotes a fine example of this self-centric one-upmanship. A neighbour was told of the overnight death of a local man by the man's son. 'Oh dear,' she said. 'How awful. That is sad. Mind you, I had a shocking night myself …'

## 135 Forgetting that ten holiday snaps for display are eight too many

## 136 Falling into the conversational gender divide

Despite living in the twenty-first century, unless the party's in a gay bar, social gatherings still tend to split along gender lines, with men at one end of the room and women at the other. Although I personally have the conversational skills of a barn owl (wide-eyed and silent) I find it even more difficult to talk to men—if you want to talk sport, you'd have better luck chatting to the sofa. I envy women their seeming ability to talk about anything with equal ease and commitment and as long as they require nothing more of me than to stare and hoot occasionally, I find their end of the room more welcoming.

What does this conversational divide say about the ineffective? Obviously, there are plenty of us about.

## 137 Forgetting people's names

A friend of mine's father once forgot his own name and was belatedly rescued from social awkwardness by his wife providing it for him. Plainly, nervousness got the better of him but even the most relaxed ineffective person can find remembering other people's names a struggle. Politicians have no such difficulty; should they uncharacteristically forget a name, they extract it effortlessly. The rest of us just stand there and panic, unable to introduce our partners who stare blankly, revelling in our discomfort and refusing to help by introducing themselves.

There are various strategies for remembering names but I can never remember them. You could try wearing a name label and pointing to it with a self-deprecating laugh while saying 'Well this is me—obviously!' At this point, the other person (no doubt wondering when the labels were provided and why they weren't given one) should answer with their own name and a similar laugh. If they don't, leave.

### 138 Failing to adequately monitor personal hygiene

The impact of a first impression cannot be over-estimated. Rightly or wrongly, we make a qualitative judgement about anyone we meet in the first thirty seconds. It can be based on anything from their clothing to their accent or the length of their eyebrows but more often than not, we use our sense of smell. Body odour or bad breath immediately mark you down as someone to be avoided. Yet how do we tell a friend or loved one that they hum? Difficult. Perhaps a birthday gift pack of Listerine might do the trick, or pass on some research that ti-tree oil and clove deodorant just doesn't cut it in today's world of rising temperatures.

### 139 Confusing an acquaintance for a friend

Friendship is an evolutionary process that grows as slowly as the mighty oak; acquaintances spring up like mustard cress. Don't burden acquaintances with the obligations of friendship, like emotional counselling or shifting your furniture. Only a friend will want to know about the strange burning sensation you get when you sit down; no acquaintance, other than your medical practitioner, needs that level of information.

## 140  Focusing your interpersonal relationships on sex

If it works, then fine—go for it, you tiger! But let's be honest here: the modern obsession with sexuality is becoming painful. The former poet laureate Sir John Betjeman was asked at the end of his life if he had any regrets. He answered: 'Not enough sex.' Hardly surprising, given that traditionally the role of poet laureate has rarely been considered to be a chick magnet. But I'm sure he's not alone in that regret; obviously, sex is a joyous and wondrous part of life, if my memory serves me correctly.

However, as fully developed individuals, once we have passed the rutting years of youthful abandon, it might be better to regard sex as something that evolves from relationships, rather than the other way round. If you want a partnership that lasts beyond breakfast, get to know what's above the waistline first. Once in a relationship, sex assumes a different role—it becomes more of a walk-on than a juvenile lead. As one wit observed: 'The good thing about being married is that you know you'll have sex. Eventually.'

## 141  Confusing pornography with eroticism

It's been said that pornography is the new rock and roll; obviously things have changed since Buddy Holly and the Crickets. Essentially a solitary pursuit for the end user, as it were, pornography has proliferated (thanks to the marvellous internet) to assume a function of vicarious polygamy;

adherents can be unfaithful in thought if not action. While not wanting to enter a moral debate on the subject, can I point out that like so much of adult-oriented drama, pornography has little to do with reality. In the real world, activity of that complex and malleable a nature involves hospitalisation. Pornographic stars (if stars is an apt word) are in it for the money, it's not done for love like amateur theatre. And don't fall for the line about the empowerment of women's sexuality; that was thought up by a man and even then he had to use a dictionary.

And do remember: in a social or work context, not everyone may share your enthusiasm for a three-way.

## 142 Finding too much time for 'Me'

People who find the time to say they never have enough time for themselves in fact probably do.

## ROLE MODELS FOR THE INEFFECTIVE

*Number 4*

BURKE AND WILLS, the Australian explorers, are two names synonymous with ineffectiveness, possessing, as they did, character shortcomings and skills-oriented inadequacies that led to a painful and untimely death in the wilderness. They were the wrong men in the wrong place at the wrong time, remembered for all the wrong reasons. Apart from that, they didn't do too bad.

Buoyed by the immense wealth generated by the Australian gold rushes in the mid-nineteenth century, the recently created Royal Society of Victoria decided to mount the Victorian Explorating Expedition, an attempt to make the first south–north land crossing of the Australian continent. In an ideal world, the expedition would then make the return north–south crossing so they could tell everybody back home all about it. The glory-hungry colony was keen for the expedition to beat its main rival, the South Australian explorer John McDouall Stuart, to the prize of £2000 being offered by the South Australian government to the first team to make the Gulf of Carpentaria and back.

The Victorians selected nineteen men for the job, to be led by Robert O'Hara Burke, a thirty-nine year old of Irish stock who had served as a cavalry officer in the Austrian army before emigrating to Australia in 1853, eventually becoming the superintendent of police in the Castlemaine district. He had no previous exploring experience and owed his appointment more to personal patronage than the skills required for the task. Likewise, his third-in-command, William John Wills, knew little of the explorer's arts—it was a fairly esoteric science even then as not many explorers returned from expeditions to pass on the trade—but he had been a shepherd, which might come in handy, and was trained as a surveyor and an astronomer.

The expedition was sent off with much pomp and ceremony from Melbourne's Royal Park on 20 August 1860. The early signs were not good; one of the wagons broke down even before it had left the park and two more collapsed before they reached suburban Essendon, where the expedition made its first overnight camp. They were ridiculously over-equipped. Along with the six wagons, twenty-three horses and twenty-seven camels, they carried twenty gallons of rum to be used as stimulants to revive the camels; a specially made branding iron to burn the letters B/VE into tree trunks at camping sites when a penknife would have done the job; enema syringes, when a penknife would have done the job; inflatable cushions, presumably for the after-effects of the enema syringes; six tonnes of firewood; a Chinese gong and a cedar-topped oak camp table—in all, the equipment weighed more than twenty tonnes!

As they laboured across Victoria, the decision was made to jettison much of the equipment. In October, the camel handler and second-in-command, George James Landells, resigned from the group after a row with Burke, who had insisted they ditch the camel's rum. The camels, by now alcohol dependent, weren't too keen on the idea either. A few days later the expedition's surgeon, Hermann Beckler, resigned as well, although it's unclear whether his departure was camel or rum-related. Sensing things weren't going fabulously, Burke decided to split the group in two, taking eight men to Coopers Creek and leaving the others to bring the rest of the equipment, including the enema syringes, at a more leisurely pace.

Feeling his rival Stuart breathing down his neck, Burke abandoned the original plan of sitting out the hot summer in Coopers Creek and struck north for the Gulf of Carpentaria in December 1860. He took with him Wills, John King and Charles Gray (so they'd have an even numbered place setting for dinner) along with six camels, one horse and enough food for only three months, four if they didn't have seconds. They reached the coast—well, within a few kilometres, the swamps being impassable—and then turned toward home. The wet season struck and the camels slowly dropped of exhaustion; three were shot and eaten while Billy the horse met his untimely end by the Diamantina River on 10 April 1861. One week later, Charles Gray died of dysentery. Having decided not to eat him, the weak and hungry remaining three explorers spent a day burying their companion.

The delay proved to be fatal. Arriving back at Coopers Creek base camp on 21 April, they found it abandoned. Brahe and his men, running low on supplies and thinking Burke and his companions would never return, had left the camp only nine hours before, leaving behind some buried provisions and instructions on the now famous 'Dig Tree'. Exhausted and unable to catch up, Burke decided they would stay and recuperate before heading for the closest pastoral settlement at Mount Hopeless, 240 kilometres away through the desert. Leaving a note of their intentions buried under the Dig Tree, they left three days later.

Meanwhile, Brahe had caught up with the other team in the expedition, who had struggled to bring the remaining supplies, including the inflatable cushions, from Menindee to Coopers Creek. Three men had died of malnutrition in the attempt. They returned to the Dig Tree at Coopers Creek on 8 May and, having spent a mere fifteen minutes looking about the place, decided that Burke had not returned—his note remained buried and unread.

Burke, Wills and King abandoned their attempt to reach Mount Hopeless as entirely hopeless and returned to the Dig Tree on 30 May. The local indigenous people, the Yandruwandha, gave them food, although Burke foolishly refused the offer of a fish on the grounds that it would make him look inferior. The explorers survived instead on ngardu, a type of damper made from the ground seeds of a native fern. Unknown to them, if prepared the wrong way, ngardu contains thiaminase which depletes the body of B1, and no doubt contributed to their deaths. Burke died at the end of June 1861, Wills a day later. King survived with the local Aborigines and was recovered two and a half months later by a rescue expedition led by Alfred William Howitt. His health broken, he died nine years later at the age of thirty-one.

There was much outpouring of grief and erection of memorial statuary for the fallen heroes in their adopted city of Melbourne. Books and films have been written about the hapless expedition and the Dig Tree is still alive today, a popular destination for outback tourists. In a sense, Burke and Wills succeeded—they did indeed make the first south–

north crossing of the continent but sadly failed to make the welcome dinner for their return. Theirs is a tragedy of near misses—to have arrived just nine hours late in the vastness of space and time that is the Australian desert truly defines Sod's Law. But had they only rid themselves of a few habits of the ineffective, who knows? They might still be with us today, albeit rather old.

### 143 Not being qualified for the job

Burke couldn't explore his way to the post office. He got the gig on who he knew, not what he knew. Some 150 years later, nothing has changed. Look at the CVs of any number of CEOs and see how many golden handshakes, exit packages and hush allowances they've had to negotiate for themselves because they're simply not up to the job. Nothing succeeds like well-disguised failure.

### 144 Relying on pack-animals with a history of substance abuse

It could be that Landells actually wanted the rum for himself and was using the camel-stimulant story as a cover. In which case, never rely on a pack-animal handler with a history of substance abuse.

### 145 Not sticking to a plan

This is one of the commonest traps for the ineffective, dashing the endeavours of so many for as long as humans have walked the planet. If history teaches us anything, it's that history teaches most of us nothing.

## 146 Not pre-soaking your ngardu seeds

If Burke had only listened to the indigenous people, he'd have realised that thousands of years of trial and error had led them to the important discovery that pre-soaking your ngardu seeds leaches away the damaging thiaminase. Wills's diaries show that he was aware the food was satiating but not nutritious; what he didn't realise was that in its un-soaked state it was giving them beri-beri. That was the price they paid for ignoring the local knowledge—either that or the local Aborigines didn't let on because they were getting their own back for the fish insult.

## 147 Packing too much for a trip

Whether it's a weekend away at the Gold Coast or a 4000 kilometre death march through the desert, never over-pack your equipment. As a good rule of thumb, pack your suitcase (or bullock dray), then remove half of the contents—you won't need it. What were they thinking when they packed the flags, rockets and two oak armchairs? And you—do you really need the *Michelin Guide to the Gold Coast* and the thermal sleeping bag in case the weather takes a turn for the worse?

# 12
# ON THE HOME FRONT

'Home is where you come to when you have nothing
better to do.'
*Margaret Thatcher*

Nothing to see here.

Gosh, Mater, love you too! Now many would argue that Margaret Thatcher was a highly effective person, seeing as she was prime minister of Great Britain and personally won the Falklands War. The what? Exactly. It was a tiny footnote of history, as windblown and desolate as Port Stanley or Goose Green. Where? Exactly.

She may have had her moment in the sun but what the Iron Lady obviously failed to realise is that for most of us, the home is where we come to when there's *too much* better to do. Once that front door closes on the outside world, we can stop pretending. It's where we can best be ourselves, and shed any masquerade of being a capable, efficient or mildly useful member of society.

It follows as surely as night follows day that the home is a hotbed of ineffectiveness, from grossly inadequate parenting skills through culinary failure to complete ineptitude in the do-it-yourself department. To err is human; to err repeatedly just makes us more human.

## PESKY HOUSEHOLD CHORES

The failure to clean up has to be one of the greatest causes of tension, distress and relationship breakdown in homes, shared households and workplaces. When you walk into an office tearoom and see a laminated sign hanging next to the Insta-boil hot water service reading: 'Your mother doesn't work here: CLEAN UP after yourself! This means YOU!!!', take the advice. (Or ask your mother to apply for a job in the same office.) In the marital home, as women have seized on the inroads into equality made by the early feminists—no, seriously—the sharing of the domestic cleaning burden has become an increasingly burning issue. In shared households, it remains the biggest single cause of dissent after bill-splitting, phone use and drinking the last of the milk.

Here are a few bombs that the ineffective trigger in the minefield of domestic ineptitude ...

### 148  Not picking up after yourself

You expect it of five year olds, not of adults. But just like five year olds, this habit can be incredibly annoying, almost as bad as teeth grinding or snoring, or being a five year old who does both. Leaving your shoes where you kick them off, a dirty plate on the table or putting the toothpaste tube with the lid off on the cistern might seem like a little thing to do, but do it every day for twenty years and you're looking at divorce. Even if you live alone it's a bad habit—how often do you spend hours searching for keys or sunglasses that you 'left just there'? Everything in its place and a place for everything.

### 149  Assigning one place as the place for everything

**150 Believing towels dry just as well on the floor**

**151 Thinking bathmats dry even better on the floor**

**152 Not cleaning the grill**

This is the domestic version of the old Buddhist conundrum: if a tree falls in the forest when no one is there to hear it, does it make a sound? If the grill lies hidden where no one can see it, does the grease harden into a bio-organic crust that resists the scouring of a thousand Big Boy pan cleaners? Yes, grasshopper. Closing the grill door and giving the fascia a quick once-over with the Spray'n'Wipe does not constitute cleaning.

**153 Leaving the dishes until morning**

Another no-no, almost up there with 'I'll just leave these to soak.' No matter how much you crave the pillow, wash the dishes before you retire for the night because the job will be ten times as ghastly to face in the morning. And you won't be stuck in bed all day waiting for your partner to make the first move so he or she (who are we kidding?—it's invariably the she) can be the first one to confront the horror. Same goes for dishwashers; make sure you stack 'n' set before you slumber or you'll be drinking your morning coffee out of the cat's dish because there are no clean mugs.

**154 Leaving dishes to drain—permanently**

**155 Ignoring small pools of stagnant water on the draining board**

**156 Failing to rinse out the dish cloths**

## 157  Tidying by piles

Not the sort of piles that can ruin a cycling tour of the Netherlands, no, these exponentially proliferate around the house. Rather than being put away, stuff is stacked into neat piles which are then placed artistically on every available surface. When I worked as a domestic cleaner to get me through university (well, it bought me three textbooks; the pay was lousy) we in the trade knew this as 'faux' tidying. It was an integral part of the Appreciable Difference, which was usually given the finishing touch by a spray of Mr Sheen into the air to give a room that 'just cleaned' fragrance. Eventually, a mathematical tipping point is reached when the sum of the piles exceeds the sum of the goods and chattels you own. The piles must now be dismantled to find something to wear, or something to write on, or indeed, your house.

## 158  Not changing the vacuum cleaner bag

## 159  Not knowing what a vacuum cleaner bag is

## 160  Having a cupboard full of unopened cleaning products

This is due to a naïve optimism washing over you as you stalk the cleaning products aisle in the supermarket (see below). The Australian non-fiction publishing sensation of 2006 was a book of household cleaning tips; the second biggest selling book was a volume by the same authors on how to clean a house more quickly. Obviously we feel a deep-seated psychological need to tackle problem stains NOW! Thankfully, the petrochemical industry has heeded our collective cry for help. There is a patented cleaning application for every facet of modern life, from mouldy bathroom grout to those tricky places to reach under the toilet rim. Lacking a degree in biochemistry as I do, it may be presumptuous of me to assume they all do largely the same thing with varying degrees of causticity. But, as a rule of thumb, one or two basic cleaning agents will get any job done with liberal applications of elbow grease. Yes, the downside is that they still require a physical application; simple purchase and wishful thinking is not enough.

## 161 Thinking that taking a shower cleans the shower receptacle

## 162 Believing that lemon juice and vinegar make a universal cleaner

In the brave new world of eco-awareness, there are those zealots who will have you believe that the juice of half a lemon mixed with white vinegar will clean anything. Perhaps it will if left to soak on the stain for fifty years. Admittedly, this simple mixture will leave your whitegoods sparkling (and smelling like a martini bar five hours after closing time) but in today's world of industrial strength filth, sometimes you need a little extra chemical back-up.

However, steer clear of the anti-bacterial wipes. This is another of the great marketing cons of the modern era, shamelessly playing on our misplaced fear of bacteria that borders on the paranoid. Despite having roughly 1000 trillion bacteria happily chomping away in and over our bodies at any given moment, more than a thousand varieties in our stomachs synthesising vitamins and fermenting complex carbohydrates, and a few billion stinkers in our armpits, we unfairly regard these sub-microscopic organisms as the enemy. Admittedly, some of the pathogenic bacteria can cause cholera, syphilis, leprosy, TB or bubonic plague—they can even give you a sore throat—but most of these single-celled pals are helpful, not only keeping our bodies functioning but breaking down the soil and waste, enabling plants to secure nitrogen and giving us cheese, yoghurt and, most importantly, beer.

Exposure to bacteria strengthens your immune system. Studies have shown that children growing up in rural areas have greater immunity to many diseases because they are exposed to the less savoury aspects of life on the farm, like drought and foreclosure. While it may not be advisable to bathe in pig excrement, it's equally foolish to try and rid your home of bacteria. For a start, it's impossible because these things can multiply faster than rabbits force-fed Viagra, and they like nothing better than a warm, moist surface, preferably a kitchen work bench or bread board that's just been wiped with a damp Chux. Personal hygiene and sensible food storage and preparation are far better protection against bad bacteria.

### 163 Writing 'Clean Me' in the soap scum on a shower screen

### 164 Believing a well-directed stream is an effective toilet cleaner

### 165 Quoting Quentin Crisp: 'There is no need to do any housework at all. After the first four years the dirt doesn't get any worse.'

This is asking to be pole-axed with a Dustbuster. Those who disdain housework are always the first to enjoy its benefits.

These are people who enjoy the comforts of crisply laundered sheets, good food and clean clothes yet wouldn't know a bottle of fabric softener if it hit them between the eyes. Which it often does.

## ELSEWHERE AROUND THE HOUSE

In the bathroom, the ineffective may be guilty of some or all of the following.

**166 Rolling toilet paper towards the wall**

**167 Leaving one frayed sheet for the next user**

**168 Showering for more than four minutes**

**169 Clearing sinuses in the shower—or worse, in the bath**

**170 Failing to activate the exhaust fan at critical moments**

**171 Weighing yourself on the scales but allowing five kilos for the underpants and T-shirt**

**172 Re-using dental floss**

Agreed, we all have to make sacrifices for the sake of the planet but there are limits.

**173 Using the face cloth for a quick wipe-over of the vanity**

**174 'Saving' water by not rinsing the sink out after shaving**

## 175  Buying a triple-headed razor

How close do you chaps want the shave to be? In their ceaseless quest to re-market the razor blade, Gillette and Co. are fast approaching hyperbole. These beard-slaying monsters are taking off skin layers, not just bristle. Still, handy for the leg shaver of either sex wanting thinner looking calves.

## 176  Borrowing a toothbrush to clean out your triple-headed razor

## 177  Breaching the his 'n' hers cabinet storage delineation

This is a growing problem with the emergence of the male metrosexual, whose thirst for skincare products cannot be sated. Traditionally, in a male–female relationship, bathroom cabinet storage was assigned on a 90/10 split, with shaving accessories, Old Spice and soap-on-a-rope jammed into one tight corner and half the Estee Lauder catalogue slewed over the rest. But the modern male preoccupation with appearance, last seen in the glory days of the Regency buck, has engineered a dramatic shift in the equation. Twin-sinked vanities are becoming commonplace and they're not called vanities without a reason. The number of male colognes—perfumes, not to put too fine a point on it—available has grown tenfold and men are increasingly being targeted to moisturise, exfoliate and buff.

Studies have repeatedly shown that skincare products are largely useless; plain Sorbolene will do the job just as well, but somehow an odourless grease lacks the *je ne sais quoi* of exotic cosmetics from Paris and New York via a sweatshop in the Philippines. A more effective skin-care regime is to drink plenty of fluids, escape the force of gravity and never grow old.

## 178  Having a cupboard crammed with alternative health products

I can never understand why people are happy to put something into their system that is promoted as 'Not tested on any living thing'. Call me selfish, but personally I'd rather not be the guinea pig. Popular herbal remedy through the ages, it may well be; but blood-letting and witchcraft were equally popular for much of the ages. Even the Chinese medical system, venerated for its ancient wisdom and traditions, still holds to the quaint notion that crushed tiger penis will improve your sexual prowess, though it does little or nothing for the tiger's.

The rush to alternative therapies is symptomatic of a contemporary reluctance to accept the fact that we're all on the way out. Despite all evidence to the contrary, we want to believe that we can feel permanently healthy; we refuse to acknowledge that, like all life forms, we reach a certain point and then inevitably decay. A sense of chronic un-wellness is perfectly natural. It's natural to not feel 100 per cent. In fact, feeling chipper is just like the elusive Happiness—it sneaks up on you, you can't plan for it, no sooner do you realise you've got it than it's gone again and you're back to feeling just a bit off. It's all in the genes, I'm afraid, and there's little you can do to alter the fact.

In the Middle Ages, the snake oil salesman peddled his wares to those desperate to see their thirtieth birthday. Modern medicine (which is not modern at all, evolving as it has over thousands of years) has largely taken care of that, but it can't provide a permanent state of vitality, so we seek the sellers of today's snake oil in the vain hope of joyously springing out of bed to greet the sun.

You may consider yourself ineffective if you unquestioningly believe in one or more of the following:

Aromatherapy
Auras
Colour Therapy
Iridology
Cleansing diets
Colonic irrigation
Tantric massage
Vitamin supplements
Chiropractic treatments for irritable bowel syndrome
Herbs to cure cancer
Bowen Therapy
Reiki.

Still, a note of caution: never underestimate the power of the placebo effect.

Meanwhile, trouble is brewing in the laundry ...

## 179 Failing to master the cycles of a washing machine

Clothes washing is one of those domestic chores that can so often provoke a household argument. Not only about who does it, but about why it needs to be done so frequently. Odd that it's a man who invariably arrives to repair a washing machine, yet so few men know how to use one. Decades after the birth of the feminist movement, comprehension of machinery still largely follows the age-old sexist divisions of domestic labour—men know cars, mowers and hedge trimmers; women know washing machines, vacuum cleaners and irons. Why is it so?

## 180 Not separating coloureds from whites

It was a very bad idea in South Africa but in the laundry apartheid makes perfect sense, unless you want to play cricket in pinks.

## 181 Failing to clean lint filters

## 182 Ironing clothes while wearing them

## 183 Drying wet clothes with a hair dryer

## 184 Hanging on to old clothes in the hope that they'll come back into fashion.

There is no point in having a wardrobe full of clothes you last wore when Princess Diana still walked among us. By the time cheesecloth comes back in, you're going to be the shape and size of a gouda and no one's going to be wanting to see even a suggestion of what's underneath your peasant blouse. And that goes for you women, too.

## 185 Thinking there are only two settings on an iron: on and off

## 186 Ironing sheets and tea-towels

While I'm the first to appreciate the beauty of a crisply laundered and pressed pillowcase as my head crashes to meet its tender embrace, life is too short to iron sheets. The ineffective also have a problem with fitted sheets—no matter how many times I have been instructed in the art of folding a fitted sheet, I can never remember the procedure. It's remarkable how the brain has evolved to block out the completely pointless.

Tea-towels should never be ironed, unless they're so badly creased that you can't read what's on them—those amusing or informative texts like 'The Scots Invented Everything' or 'Rules of this Kitchene'.

### 187  Using a laundry service

Now you might think you're being effective: good use of time management through outsourcing of menial chore, saving on depreciation and running costs of equipment while creating employment opportunity for illegal immigrants. No, you're just being a lazy, patronising sod.

And things aren't much better in the lounge/family/rumpus/media/whatever room/den/nook either …

### 188  Monopolising the remote control

### 189  Believing that cable television will improve your life

### 190  Being the first on the block to buy new technology

In many ways, we should be grateful to the early-uptakers of new technologies because they quickly filter out those innovations doomed to the scrapheap. These are the people who bought the eight-track cartridges, the rear-projection televisions, the digital cassette players, the CD-ROM encyclopaedias and the home frozen-yoghurt makers. Occasionally, something slips through the net, like the VHS video format that usurped the superior BETA tape, or the Windows operating system. But by and large, resist the temptation to jump on the techno bandwagon immediately because prices will inevitably fall and quality improve.

## 191  Desperately trying to impress visitors with a home theatre system

'Listen—the seagull noise comes out behind your left ear! Amazing isn't it?' To a point, yes, but the really amazing thing is you fell for the line from some clever executive at Sony or Phillips who thought: 'We could sell millions of these things to people who want to pretend they're in the cinema when they're really just stuck at home watching a big TV. As long as they don't remember they've only got two ears!'

Surround sound, Sensurround, Panavision, Smell-o-Vision, 3-D —they were all format tweaks designed to get you back into the movie theatres. Home theatre systems are format tweaks designed to get you back into the electronics department stores. We listen to the world in stereo, being blessed as we are with stereophonic listening devices, one on either side of our heads, called ears. Our hearing range is low relative to others in the animal kingdom and our ears are firmly anchored in the one direction; unlike a cat, we can't twist our ears to pick up sounds behind us. A good stereo sound system will spatially reproduce the way we aurally perceive the world. The rest is merely bells and whistles, hiding the fact that while the delivery system changes, forcing you to open your wallet to keep up, the content remains depressingly the same.

## 192 Watching too much TV

How much is too much? Some would say simply turning it on has a detrimental effect; others champion the medium as providing the social glue that holds the globalised world together. Despite the growth of the internet, television remains the single most powerful media force in the world. Like the internet, it creates a sense of ersatz community; its greatest strength is the commonality of experience, a show or event we'll all talk about the next day or in the years to come. As with popular music, TV has provided generational defining moments in our lives—largely, it must be said, in the late adolescent years. It's difficult to predict how long television can sustain this for; as the world increasingly seeks novelty, the shared experience fractures and becomes evermore ephemeral.

## 193 Watching exercise programs

## 194 Subscribing to the Lifestyle Channel

As one American wit put it: 'Anyone who uses the word lifestyle has neither.' Lifestyle, travel and shopping channels are mind-sapping black holes operating on a culture of envy that will destroy you. There, I've said it.

## IN THE KITCHEN

The kitchen should be the epicentre of any well-regulated home—a place to meet, to cook and break bread together, to exchange ideas and experience the ebb and flow of family life. It's a worrying modern trend that a microwave oven, a fridge and a sink is often considered to constitute a modern kitchen—too many times it's little more than the resting place of limp celery and expired milk, a fluttering note pinned to the refrigerator door saying: 'Gone out. Back some time.'

Increasingly, we live vicariously in the kitchens of others; food preparation has become a spectator sport as we gaze into the domestic hearths of Delia Smith, Nigella Lawson or Martha Stewart before she did time in the big house and her kitchen was a dank hall filled with industrial appliances where she fought off lesbians wielding heavy-duty blending wands. There is no evidence to suggest that these cooking shows have made us cook more ourselves. Indeed, the highly ineffective, if they have a functioning kitchen at all, continue to make a few fundamental mistakes.

## 195 Buying recipe books for the pictures

For a long time, cooking was drudgery born of necessity. Anyone who has had to put a meal on the table every night knows how relentlessly tedious—and mentally challenging—it can be. It's another of those repetitive chores that threatens to paralyse decision making. You might be able to run a business but trying to think of something to make for dinner ten times on the trot can be as difficult as rowing across the Atlantic. French philosopher Montaigne was right when he observed 'There is scarcely any less bother in the running of a family than in that of an entire state. And domestic business is no less importunate for being less important.' (I've looked up 'importunate' in the dictionary for you; it means pressing or persistent.) And he said that in the sixteenth century, long before the invention of the George Foreman health grill or the fan-forced oven.

With the advent of convenience foods, the pressure on the home chef was momentarily lifted, until the appeal of Rosella Savoury Rice paled and cooking found itself a new niche as recreational pastime. Professional cooks entered the world of publishing and the commercial recipe book suddenly became an essential ingredient in finding and preparing any essential ingredients. Look in a bookshop and see how big the cookbook section is; it almost rivals the other escapist departments of Travel or New Age Health. Food looks fantastic in cookbooks, good enough to eat, but don't kid yourself that your Angel Hair Pasta with Thai Baked Prawns is going to look anything like it does in the glossy picture. Even with luck, the best it's going to do is bear an uncanny resemblance to three limp mandarin segments in a nest of pubic hair.

A much better bet than attempting a dish out of *Authentic Szechuan Cooking* or *Flavours of Tuscany* is to buy a book that recognises you for what you are in the kitchen: hopeless. This sort of book has simple instructions for making toast, boiling eggs or mashing potatoes. It might sound patronising—well, it is—but start with the basics and gradually work up to more complicated dishes that contain not only meat but also three veg. Photograph the results and compile your own cookbooks of family favourites, perhaps giving them interesting names like 'Old Jack's Cajun Re-fried Beans' (baked beans with HP sauce) or 'Pomme de Terre au Pre-gratin' (jacket potato with pre-grated cheese).

## 196 Serving food with the lights on

Candles were invented for a reason; keep the light low, keep them guessing.

## 197 Using blunt knives

Sounds so straightforward, doesn't it? But how many of us have hacked away at a tomato with a knife that couldn't slice through air yet never has any trouble taking the top of your finger off? Basic equipment is essential in a kitchen. Don't worry about the esoterica like olive de-stoners or butane torches for the perfect crème brûlée; they're for the try-hards who get up at 5 a.m. on a Saturday to go to the growers' market. A worktop is a good starting point but don't clutter it with manual coffee grinders and pestles. Next, buy one quality set of saucepans—and I mean quality. Department store clearance sales are an excellent source; for some mysterious reason, luggage, personal massage equipment and saucepans are always heavily marked down once every twelve months. Don't stint yourself in the blade department, you'll only spend a lot more on Band-Aids if you do. And buy a sharpener while you're at it. Just on the off-chance that you blunt the knives by actually using them.

A stove and an oven are useful and a decent food processor is a must. It looks professional and it saves a lot of chopping and grinding. Only a hopeless romantic makes pesto by hand—if Dorothy Parker didn't say that, I bet she wished she had. Wooden spoons, graters, mashers, mixing bowls and jugs can all be added gradually as your increasing skills require more specialised equipment. Don't bother with a bread-maker; the novelty of shapeless lumps with the consistency of moist concrete wears off fairly quickly.

## 198 Buying a bread maker

## 199 Hand-stuffing olives, cherry tomatoes or anything smaller than a capsicum

## 200 Microwaving pizza

Once you've equipped your kitchen, read the instruction manuals to get an idea of what each piece of apparatus does best. The microwave oven is good for defrosting, re-heating and cooking foods with a high moisture content. It is not good for crisping; pizzas, breads, pastry goods and half-eaten kebabs will not be at their best re-heated in a microwave oven. Yes, they'll be ready quickly but they'll not only have the texture of a wet flannel, they'll burn the skin off the roof of your mouth as soon as you bite into them. Similarly, the modern convection oven offers more features and cooking modes than ever before; gone are the days when you set the temperature and either put the casserole dish on the bottom or the top shelf. Some high-end ovens even come with a dial-in Help Desk so if you're in doubt about the correct setting for soufflé, you can make a two-minute noodle instead.

## 201 Not reading the instruction manual

## 202 Looking at a full fridge or pantry and saying 'There's nothing to eat.'

Unless specifically guided by bright and informative packaging, many ineffective people don't actually recognise food in its native state. They can visit a farm and mistake it for a large-scale petting zoo, albeit one with a high turnover of animal residents. Lacking a fundamental knowledge of ingredients, they also lack the imagination to combine simple foodstuffs into something tasty—they don't see that two eggs, sea salt and a handful of coarsely chopped leg ham, spring onions and vine tomatoes equals an omelette with bits in it.

This is the sort of person who can open a fridge packed with food yet find nothing to eat. Ten minutes later, they open the fridge again, vainly hoping that something's changed in the meantime. It hasn't. Five minutes after that, they're ordering take-out. Often they will binge grocery shop, hoping to solve their dilemma by replacing all the food they had with something that looks more appetising.

## 203 Buying fruit and vegetables, storing for two weeks, then throwing them away

Good intentions count for little in the kitchen. Don't buy it unless you're going to either try it, fry it or dry it. As a rule of thumb, the shorter the shelf life of food, the better it is for you, with the possible exception of dried legumes and pulses. But if you've bought a case of mangoes and have no idea what to do with them all, why not give some to neighbours—it's never too late to meet them. Make a mango smoothie with the organic yoghurt you bought on your last health kick (check the use-by date first) or combine with seasonal fruits for a delicious *salade de fruits* which you can then store in the fridge for two weeks before binning.

## 204 Not knowing how to puree apples

## 205 Buying a fruit drying and preserving kit

Excellent plan—I'll buy two crates of apricots from the growers' market then spend a leisurely Sunday drying them, or bottling the preserved fruit in pre-sterilised jars. Who are you trying to kid? The only pre-sterilised jars you've got are the ones for the urine samples you were supposed to hand in for your annual medical ten years ago and you've already booked the next ten Sundays for wardrobe clean-out, second-hand book and CD sort-out and a garage sale to clear the shed.

## 206 Buying from sales reps in supermarkets

You know the ones—set up with an electric frypan in a corner somewhere near the pet food section, wearing a name tag saying VISITOR because the supermarket doesn't want to be tainted by association. Being a cheapskate, it's hard to resist taking a sample, then heading off on a circuit of the laundry goods and light bulbs aisle before coming back, trying to look like a different customer for another handout. Then, of course, the guilt kicks in and you start feeling sorry for this retiree trying to supplement their pension with in-store promotional work so you find yourself buying two packets of organic free range turkey and mint sausages. And they taste quite nice. Of course they do! Anything free prepared by someone else tastes good! But when you get home, you discover the strange giblet aftertaste that evaded you in the supermarket and you could start your own bio-diesel business with the amount of fat that drips out of them.

## 207 Buying everything from supermarkets

In an ideal world, we'd have the time to buy our food on a daily basis, purchasing the fresh ingredients as we need them. Oddly enough, we do have the time to do just that but somewhere along the line, we all got hooked into going to the supermarket. These places might be fine for bulk goods and staples like toilet paper or tinned tomatoes but at the expense of the local grocer, fruit shop, baker, newsagent, mechanic, clothing store, bottle shop, hardware shop, petrol station and chemist, they've also cornered the market in everything else. What's next? Supermarket no-frills escort services for the lonely business gentleman?

The modern self-service supermarket began life in the United States in the early twentieth century and really took off during the Great Depression when consumers became price-sensitive—i.e. broke. Different countries around the world have embraced the supermarket in varying degrees. Great Britain has probably the strongest concentration of supermarkets, up from a few hundred in the 1950s to more than 4500 today, with four main players controlling 75 per cent of the grocery market. Projections indicate that, on current trends, there will be no independent food stores in Britain by 2050. Take a look at what's happened to butchers in the United Kingdom: 23,000 in 1985, a mere 9721 in 2000. (Hardly surprising, though, given the meat's rubbish and costs a fortune.) Local producers are either marginalised or squeezed by the big chains, with suppliers being paid as little as a tenth of the retail value of their produce and locked into supply contracts, being told exactly what and when to grow. Food is now transported vast distances—Tescos, the country's biggest grocery retailer (with 30 per cent market share), sends its lorries driving 240 million kilometres each year.

In the United States, the Wal-Mart chain has 1.5 million employees (all non-union, of course) who begin each week by singing the company song before rolling out another hypermarket in some greenfield site at the rate of one or two a week. In Australia, two supermarket chains, Woolworths and Coles, dominate 80 per cent of the dry food market—between them they sell 62 per cent of all the milk drunk in the country.

They even run poker machines—Woolies now controls nearly 11,000 of them to be the country's third-largest operator of gaming machines. A connection with groceries escapes me.

## 208 Not preparing a shopping list

These stores rely on a few basic principles to ensure their dominance, such as free parking, economies of scale, downward price pressure on suppliers, bundling other products like alcohol or petrol, or charging producers for the privilege of being stocked at all with added costs for prime shelf positions. But the primary tool is the loss leader: heavy discounting on items like bread and milk to give the often false impression that everything else in the store is equally cheap. This is known in the trade as the KVI, the Known Value Item, and it works by recognising that most shoppers have a rough idea of how much, say, a litre of milk costs, then knocking 20 per cent off that—even if it means selling the product for less than it costs to provide.

It's a psychological trick that has us all duped. Tied as we are to the notion of filling the trolley once a week or fortnight, the best thing we can do to minimise our exposure to the deceit is make a **shopping list and stick to it**. Buy what you need, not what someone else thinks you want. Avoid the impulse buy, because it's the UKVIs (the Unknown Value Items) that provide the supermarkets with their generous profits.

Indeed, whole chains have sprung up to cater for nothing but impulse buys. Ever gone into an Aldi supermarket that operates on some sort of curious Soviet-style consumer strategy, with unrelated goods piled high yet others completely missing? You might not find tea-bags in the shop but you will stumble across truss tomatoes walking out the door at fifty cents a kilo or chocolates from the Balkan states at very competitive prices. So competitive, in fact, that in a flash you forget that you're allergic to tomatoes or that chocolate with less than 3 per cent cocoa mass tastes like brown paper. Within minutes your car is piled high with the stuff. Two months later it's taking up valuable space in your garbage bin.

## 209 Thinking everything in a supermarket is cheaper or better value

## 210 Taking nine items into the eight item express lane

It's petty and demeans you as a human being. It demeans us as a race. And for the record, six tins of tuna chunks do not count as one item.

## 211 Not knowing what's actually in the food you're buying

## 212 Knowing what's actually in the food but buying it anyway

## 213 Buying snack-sized chocolate bars

A neat little trick from the manufacturers: cut-down versions of the popular varieties, ideal for the kids after school or for the diet conscious who just need a little something with a cup of tea. In reality, the kids never see them after you've ploughed through the whole packet because surely chocolate bars that tiny can't be fattening?

## 214 Buying Priced-to-Clear goods

They're priced to clear for a reason—no one else wants them. Often approaching their use-by date, or in some cases well past it, the priced-to-clear food item may be handy, provided you can consume it before you leave the store. Anything later risks botulism. Discontinued lines are another trap for the unwary. Supermarkets rely on the false impression that they are a cornucopia of choice. A discontinued line means that even they couldn't find enough consumers who wanted to try sparkling mineral water infused with cumquat, or Swiss cheese without the holes.

## 215 Buying food marked 'Genuine Organic'

Doubtless it's been shipped in from some obscure foreign province where the only thing organic about it is the human excrement sprayed on it to make it grow. The organic food revolution is being seized upon by the unscrupulous while the regulatory authorities are still catching up. Bowing to market pressure, the big supermarkets are sourcing 'organic' produce themselves, or even forming alliances with local growers' markets to green their own credentials, allowing a few motley stalls in the car park on weekends that sell organic jam and sourdough bread. Try growing organic food yourself; it's all but impossible. No sooner have you put your parsley and rocket plants in the ground than every leaf-eating bug known to science has defoliated them. You have two choices: either sit there with a torch and defend the plants by hand, or spray something seriously lethal. You can easily recognise fresh organic fruit and vegetables in the shops—they're usually wizened, mottled and three times as expensive.

## IN THE HOME OFFICE

As we move to a deregulated workforce and the miracle of technology allows us to work from home, the home office (formerly known as a sunroom or the cupboard under the stairs and now known as a SOHO—Shithouse Office Home Office) is becoming more commonplace. Equipping and successfully running a home office is a challenge that so many more of us can now fail to meet.

## 216 Working from home to be more productive

One of the main selling points of working from home is that we'll become a lot more productive. Productive at everything else other than work, certainly. I have a friend who placed her home office at the back of the house, remote and accessible only over three stepping stones placed across an ornamental pond. She spends more time on the stepping stones than anywhere else, to-ing and fro-ing like a demented billygoat as another task, like boiling the kettle or rinsing lettuce, suddenly becomes more interesting. It takes exceptional self-discipline to stay in a home office for more than fifteen minutes at a time. Distractions are endless and, unlike a conventional working environment, all human interaction is tangential—like a visit from the postman, the cleaner or the complete stranger you drag in off the street because you're so desperately lonely. Gone is the inspiration of the collegiate—the sharing of ideas and the discipline and competition of your peers.

If you have children under the age of twelve, abandon the home office idea altogether. Not only will they distract you, you'll always run out of sticky tape and your stapler will never be where you left it. Your cheque book with be filled with 'Pay: ME One million dollars' and your appointments calendar marked with the birthdays of the Saddle Club.

## 217 Purchasing a whyteboard to generate ideas

Bad news—whyteboards don't generate ideas, you do. A clean, crisp whyteboard promises so much, a world of limitless potential that soon collapses under the paucity of accomplishment you bring to it. Einstein formulated the theory of relativity working as a clerk in the patents office. If he'd bought a whyteboard and stayed at home, he'd probably have come up with a list of titles recommended on Oprah's Book Club.

## 218 Over-equipping

Sure, it's hopeless trying to run an effective, creative career with one phone, a chair and a typewriter—how on earth did Ernest Hemingway manage it? But equally ineffective is the gadget-freak who buys everything going at Officeworks. CEO leatherette chairs with five-way movement or an all-in-one printer/scanner/fax/auto-collating photocopier/PABX/voicemail with optional blood pressure monitor. Think about it—can something be really so cheap and do even half of all that well? And what have you got to hide, other than your weight loss diary, that needs a document shredder?

## 219 Equipping ergonomically

Sounds good, and within reason it can be useful. But the ergonomic balls won't last five minutes. Ditto the yoga mat, Pilates equipment and foot massager.

## 220 Not handling paper once

The idea of 'handle paper once' is a concept quite beautiful in its simplicity. Whenever you receive a piece of paper—be it bill, letter to respond to, memo or whatever—do all that it requires you to do immediately. If it's a bill, pay it, note the receipt and file it in the one fluid action. If it's a letter that needs a response, respond, envelope and attach a stamp now. If it's an invoice, either pay it or return with 'Not Known at this Address' now.

## 221 Mistaking a box for a filing cabinet

## 222 Mistaking a filing cabinet for a box

If you have a filing cabinet, use it properly. Don't let it become a receptacle for things like spare spectacles, the neighbour's keys, your last will and testament and the first father's day card you got from the kids. Buy the correct sized files and labels and divide into appropriate categories—neither too generalised nor too specific. File in alphabetical or numerical order and cull the contents every six months, disposing of files no longer valid, like 'Potential Contacts', 'Film Script Ideas' or 'Concluded Sales'.

## 223 Not keeping an accurate diary

Have you ever noticed that effective people rarely keep their own diaries? They have someone to do that for them, briskly following them about with perky reminders of the two-thirty. You can now keep an electronic diary and upload it to your Blackberry, your laptop and via worldwide web to any desktop on earth. This means that you can now forget a meeting in a vast number of ways. The secret of diary keeping is to not only **write** in it but to also **read** it.

Don't be afraid to carry a paper diary. Scientists have shown that the human brain actually comprehends less from a pixelated document on the screen than one written on paper; a screen image oscillates as it reaches and is received by the optic nerve. An image printed on paper, on the other hand, doesn't oscillate, unless your hands are shaking from a big one the night before. Paper diaries may not look as cool but they have several other advantages: they're laid out in a manner spatially more in tune with the way the human mind processes chronological information and they cost nothing to run.

## 224 Not keeping simple and accurate accounts

Even Gandhi did it. There are many home book-keeping software packages available but even the simplest can be overly complicated for the average user. Work out an accounting system you can run in an exercise book then set up the same functions in your computerised accounts. At least it will look professional—and should you run into difficulties with the tax office, hide.

## 225 Setting up an alternative medicine facility in your own home

Plenty of these around. You can smell the patchouli as you walk past and hear the ambient dolphin song leaking out of the front door to mingle with the Buddhist wind chimes scattered about the drought-proof garden of hardy natives. Once inside, you glance at the walls; if she can look at all the colours on a Dulux chart and still pick that one, what the hell is she going to do to my back? The mail-order diploma in the Ikea frame does little to inspire confidence, as does the portable massage table that groans under your weight as you assume the position.

The music is changed to waterfalls mixed with exotic birds and you feel the warm towel descend. 'Tense today,' comes a quiet voice as oiled hands move over you, interrupted by muted requests from the family on the other side of the curtain and the odd door slamming in the distance. An hour later, the only weight lifted off your shoulders is the $90 you were carrying in your wallet when you arrived.

## 226  Over-stocking the beverage and biscuits facilities

Tea and coffee facilities in the home office can be a tax deduction but don't overdo it. You'll spend more time at the espresso machine and the friand maker than you will at your desk, and no amount of rolling on your ergonomic balls is going to shift those kilojoules.

## ROLE MODELS FOR THE INEFFECTIVE

*Number 5*

SIR CLIVE SINCLAIR is a British inventor and electronics trailblazer, responsible for designing and manufacturing many miniature radios, calculators, electric cars and folding bikes, as well as introducing the first home computer in the UK to be sold under £100. Born in 1940 into a family of engineers in Richmond-upon-Thames, Clive became interested in electronics at an early age, tinkering away at amplifiers, radios, communications systems and other nerdish products with like-minded chums at his local school. His father suffered a business setback when he decided to import miniature tractors from the United States; sadly he had failed to foresee the lack of miniature farmers in the UK domestic market and soon went broke. As the family moved about the country looking for employment and other possible miniature tractor applications, Clive became increasingly independent, publishing his first electronics research article while still at school. He decided against going to university, pursuing instead those subjects of interest that he could teach himself.

He found a job as an editorial assistant for an electronics magazine and also began selling his own miniature electronics kits by mail order. Combining innovation with a salesman's flair, in 1961 Clive created the company Sinclair Radionics with the corporate philosophy of providing budget electronic goods for the mass market, often sold in kit form. Sharing his father's fascination with miniaturisation, he created the world's first compact pocket calculator, the Sinclair Executive, in 1972. It was no wider than a packet of cigarettes—in fact, the width of a cigarette packet was the overriding design brief dimension of much that the company manufactured, largely because back then Clive puffed his way through forty fags a day.

Eight years later, he gave the world the first budget home computer, the ZX80, and two years later, the TV80 flat screen TV. The ZX81 soon followed and in 1984, shortly before the groundbreaking Apple Macintosh went on sale, Clive announced the Sinclair QL computer. It was a much more complicated machine than its predecessors but unfortunately was under-developed and under-powered, with problems in manufacture that saw demand initially outstripping supply, Even worse, supply soon outstripped demand and the project lost a fortune. Still, the early home computers produced by Sinclair's companies introduced a whole generation to the wonders of the digital age.

However, Sir Clive's place in the history books is more guaranteed by his high-profile failures than his successes. Being naturally inquisitive and impetuous, he has at times rushed into production of products that were not, shall we say, completely thought through. Such as the Transrista, a matchbox-sized radio that could be worn around the wrist (hence the name) and was claimed to be the smallest wireless in the world, powerful enough to pick up signals from Europe. Technically it could, but there was a slight drawback: it picked them up simultaneously, which had a dampening effect on your listening pleasure. Then there was the Black Watch, an early digital watch from 1975 that was inconveniently temperature sensitive, running at different speeds in summer and winter. The control panel often malfunctioned, making it impossible to turn off , which occasionally led to the batteries exploding. Not exactly the sort of alarm you were after.

But the lemon that topped them all was the personal pedal/electric commuter vehicle, the C5. Launched as a revolutionary alternative to the motor car, the C5 was a low-slung, three-wheeled device that left the driver exposed to the elements and at roughly the same height as the average lorry exhaust pipe. With a top speed of only 15 mph, a limited range of twenty miles (less in cold weather) and a dislike of hills, the C5 mysteriously failed to live up to the sales expectation of millions of units. In fact, it managed only 5000 worldwide, although it's now something of a collector's piece and has managed to attain cult status amongst a hardy band of enthusiasts. One C5 buff has even used a turbo-charged version of the person-mover to break the world land speed record for an electric vehicle, sending it along at 150 mph—without using the pedals.

Was the C5 the right electric vehicle in the wrong place? No—it was a complete and utter dud. Sure, Elton John owns two to drive around his estate (which is hardly surprising because Elton John buys just about anything with a price tag on it). Even so, its description as a washing-machine motor on three wheels proved unshakeable. But as the world is only slowly embracing the electric car and extraordinary personal transport inventions like the Segue struggle to make inroads, it's clear that Sir Clive and his C5 were way ahead of their time. How ironic that a man with such insight and inventiveness will be best—and unfairly—remembered as a laughing stock.

## 227 Being ahead of your time

Not something the ineffective are traditionally accused of—if anything, it's more often the reverse as they struggle to catch up. But timing is an important part in effectiveness, being in the right time at the right place is all. As Woody Allen once said, 90 per cent of success is turning up. Remembering where and when to turn up is the hard part.

## 228 Presenting something to the public before it's ready

This can be anything from a groundbreaking computer to a celebrity adopted orphan from the sub-continent—it could even be a new hair colour you're trying or maybe a rad tattoo. Just make sure it's all ready and set to go—nothing worse than rolling up your sleeve to display 'Born Looser' to the gang at work. Never forget that while the world may welcome your triumphs, it can't wait for your failures.

## 229 Inventing exploding digital watches

For a start, you couldn't get away with it these days. As soon as the thing went *kaboom*! you'd have a writ slapped on you claiming $200 million for detonated watch battery-related stress and trauma. I realise it's everyone's dream to invent something that will change the world and, more importantly, generate a lucrative royalty stream but your chances of coming up with an original idea—let alone getting it to production—are approaching absolute zero. However, if you feel you must persevere, try to limit your inventiveness to the non-fissile.

## 230  Wearing digital watches, exploding or not

Who'd be seen dead wearing a digital watch these days? It's an object lesson for the fashion or trend conscious: today's iPod is yesterday's Walkman.

# 13
# SPECIAL OCCASIONS

'A lovely thing about Christmas is that it's compulsory, like a thunderstorm, and we all go through it together.'
*Garrison Keillor*

Proceed to the next page.

There are certain occasions that define us as socially active human beings, rites of passage that mark the ebb and flow of our lives. Doubtless intended as celebratory beacons to light the darkness of existence, these red letter days heralding the memory of our birth, graduation, betrothal, farewell or return, retirement or death all figure unpleasantly in the lives of the ineffective. Perhaps it's the weight of anticipation, the sense of being judged or our inability to process alcohol efficiently that mark these rituals out as painful experiences. Any challenge in which the ineffective are asked to meet high expectations can only be wishfully described as character building. Yet harrowing as they may be, we are strangely drawn to these tribal commemorations.

The memory of last year's Christmas may make us shudder throughout the year, yet three days before the next Yuletide, the unpleasant memories mysteriously recede, along with our resolve to never repeat the experience. We happily re-marry, conveniently forgetting that our previous experiment with the institution led to seven years of lassitude and emotional distress, plus the loss of the holiday photos and half the house. Having survived the first three sleepless years of a child, we go and have another one—on purpose! Scarcely weeks after a dinner party that had all the conversational éclat of wet gravel, we happily dig out the menu planners and start making a few calls.

But in these modern times of individualism, as we become increasingly isolated in our own homes, even the receiving of visitors has in itself become a special occasion. Do you go into a mild panic when guests drop in unannounced? From having been a common social convention, the surprise visit is now on the endangered list. Who now will willingly brave the traffic and the anxiety to use their precious spare time to drive across town on the off-chance you might be in? Having friends around for a meal, once a chance to have a few drinks and a chat while breaking bread together, now requires weeks of planning, calendar cross-referencing, the sourcing of gourmet supplies and a cable-TV cooking channel subscription to make sure you get it all right.

Any social occasion has almost become the triumph of optimism over experience.

## 231 Volunteering to have the family over for Christmas

Even for millions of people who don't believe in Christmas, Christmas remains the singularly most fraught, emotional and divisive day of the year. One of the more ludicrous results of political correctness in the United States was to have Merry Christmas re-branded as Happy Holidays to avoid offending minorities who didn't share the religious belief. Why bother? Christmas offends everyone!

Dragged into the conspiracy at birth with the promise of gifts delivered by a fat man from the icy blasts of the North Pole

(Santa is a pre-global-warming phenomenon), we feel duty bound to assemble each year to distribute more stuff we don't need to people who don't want it. Even so, if someone decides to dig a well in the Sudan on our behalf or give us a jar of home-made chutney in lieu of a real present, we feel cheated.

Born as it is in childhood, at some point as we grow up responsibility for the family Christmas ritual must be passed on to the next generation. But as the next generation inevitably involves at some stage, however briefly, two separate families, this is where the problem starts. To which family do we go? Or do we offer to bring everyone together, even though we've only got eight forks and the place feels crowded when the cat comes in? Best to sit quiet until some sibling or other makes the first move and then offer to bring the salads.

**232 Buying Christmas presents on Christmas Eve from a petrol station**

**233 Resolving to buy next year's presents in the January sales**

**234 Spending more than the gift limit when no one else does**

**235 Persisting in the misguided belief that paper hats make a party zing**

**236 Volunteering to be Santa at a child-care centre**

This is a bad idea in these litigious, untrusting times. Even four year olds are wise to the unproven allegation of inappropriate behaviour. Before you know it, you'll be blackmailed into buying one of the little terrors a PlayStation because if you don't they're going straight to the supervisor to whimper 'Santa touched me in a bad way.'

## 237 Imagining that anyone will want to hear you singing carols at their door

## 238 Making fruit mince pies for the neighbours at 2.30 a.m. on 25 December

## 239 Writing gift tags from Santa in your own handwriting

## 240 Organising the office Christmas party

## 241 Attending the office Christmas party

## 242 Buying from a corporate gift registry

It remains a mystery as to how two golf balls stamped with your name and a sprig of holly ever came to be considered as a thoughtful, welcome present. Likewise, the gift basket. Its origins owing something, however remote, to the mythical horn of plenty, the gift basket offers little more than a heavily inflated price. Present the recipient with a miniscule ham, a bottle of Jacobs Creek chardonnay, a packet of water crackers and a pâté, then shower them with polystyrene beads, glitter and cellophane. Exactly the same effect at half the price.

## 243 Thinking that this New Year's Eve is going to be better than last

For some reason, we all feel a compulsive need to gather to mark the arbitrary passing of a year and welcome in the next one in the vain hope that it will be better than the twelve months we've just endured. Historical research indicates that this is unlikely to be the case but still we place ourselves in the middle of unruly, drunken crowds to watch fireworks at midnight then spend the first week of the New Year trying to find a taxi to get home. At some point in our lives, we belatedly recognise the futility of the enterprise and stay at home, watching the festivities on the television; some years later, we can't even be bothered to do that and are only barely woken from our slumbers at midnight by the blare of car horns, incomprehensible yelling and someone throwing up over our front garden.

## 244 Staying up till midnight just so you get to kiss someone. Anyone.

## 245 Making New Year's resolutions

If you recognise a need to make resolutions, why doesn't it occur to you that you can in fact make them at any time? Try making a resolution on 12 August, or revert to the old-fashioned notion of abstaining for Lent. Either has an equal chance of success. Alternatively, keep your resolutions private because: a) no one else is really interested; b) you won't feel so bad when you invariably fail to keep them; or c) it's another guilty secret you can add to your steadily growing pile of self-loathing.

## 246 Organising an Easter egg hunt

It's a curious twist of modern retailing that no sooner is the tinsel celebrating Christ's birth packed away than the shelves are groaning under the weight of chocolate eggs supposedly commemorating his demise. 'What larks,' you think as you purchase fourteen dozen Caramello eggs on the cheap from Aldi, 'I'll organise an egg hunt for the children.' After a desultory poke through the bushes, half the kids are in diabetic shock and the rest are biting each other and demanding a recount of the eggs that have been collected into one basket and re-distributed democratically so the slower kids don't have lowered self-esteem. Which is a nice thought. But honestly, it's only going to make the slow ones fatter. Six months later you're still picking up soggy eggs in the lawnmower.

## 247  Organising an Easter egg hunt with hand-painted, hard-boiled eggs

They might have been doing it in Sweden for hundreds of years but no child wants to be taught about the pagan origins of Easter with anything other than chocolate. Never volunteer to do anything 'fun but educational' for children.

## 248  Attempting to organise a wedding

A wedding is perhaps the most eagerly anticipated and frequently disappointing ritualised ceremony in many, if not all, of the world's cultures, combining as it does the promise of new beginnings with only the veiled threat of premature endings. Often the first choice of screenwriters and the saviour of many a TV series floundering in the ratings, weddings in the real world confront the ineffective with so many traps, be they attending as guests, as family, as official party, as bride or as bridegroom, presenting as they do the widest range of opportunities to make a social faux pas.

## 249  Confusing the bride with her sister or mother

Traditionally the white dress has been something of a guide but in these days of civil ceremonies it can be difficult, especially if you've only been invited by default as someone's partner.

## 250 Assuming, as best man, that everyone will laugh at what you find funny

The best real wedding speech line I've heard came not from the best man but from the father of the bride. He welcomed his new son-in-law into the family with the following glowing observation about his daughter: 'She's lucky to get you, mate—she's had more pricks in her than a second-hand dart board.' Luckily, everyone managed to see the funny side and the happy couple were divorced two years later. It's a good lesson for any potential speech giver: some things are best left unsaid.

## 251 Agreeing to wear a white suit or chiffon in any pastel shade

## 252 Thinking that a four year old in a tuxedo looks cute, especially when carrying rings on a satin cushion

## 253 Opting for matching mullet hairstyles for the groom's entourage

## 254 Saying 'It usually doesn't rain much at that time of year.'

## 255 Believing that stretch limousines are sophisticated

## 256 Allowing your mother to assume planning control

Even worse if you're the groom. Although the modern wedding requires more planning than the D-Day invasion of Europe, never allow your mother to assume control.

Remember that weddings are rarely for those getting married; the bride and groom are merely the laboratory rats in an ongoing social experiment and the ritual is primarily for the benefit of the observers. Try to keep some control over just who those observers are going to be—think of how different an experiment would be if the rats had a chance to design it.

Avoid the wedding planner. Not only will you feel like you're in a second-rate Hollywood comedy, but any vestige of personal involvement and originality will be subsumed by the wedding industrial complex that threatens to devour the ceremony of marriage, with its table centrepieces, decorative chair covers, trained doves and Cinderella marquees.

## 257 Spending longer on the wedding photos than you do on the ceremony

Often photos are the only way you'll remember any aspect of your own wedding but avoid the temptation to spend five hours being photographed standing in front of the Opera House, or whatever exceptional architectural marvel is convenient to the reception venue. Videoing the event with a three-camera shoot for a commemorative DVD is also symptomatic of the modern tendency to focus solely on the event, substituting wedding for marriage, rather than seeing it as the first tentative step on a long and difficult journey.

## 258 Buying a breadmaker as a wedding gift

## 259 Suggesting it might be a nice gesture of reconciliation to invite your ex-partner to your wedding

Special Occasions

**260** **Bringing your kids on the honeymoon**

**261** **Whispering 'Better luck this time, hey?' when you meet at the altar**

# ROLE MODELS FOR THE INEFFECTIVE

*Number 6*

NAPOLEON BONAPARTE may not immediately spring to mind as an ineffective person, seeing as he conquered most of continental Europe, instituted a code of civil law, became Emperor of France and is considered by many to be the finest military tactician that ever lived. Not a bad CV to pack into just over fifty-one years on this earth. But he had some highly ineffective habits—his work/life balance was dreadful and re-introducing slavery can only be seen as a backward step. Merely being the scourge of Europe doesn't necessarily make you a good person and, as mother always said, It's nice to be important but it's more important to be nice.

Born in Corsica in 1769, one year after the Genoese territory was handed over to France, Napoleon wasn't even technically French, coming from minor Tuscan nobility and speaking with an Italian accent throughout his life. Packed off to military school at the age of nine, he proved an able student at anything to do with guns (although spelling proved beyond him, even into adulthood) and was made a second lieutenant in the artillery at the tender age of sixteen.

After the revolution of 1789, Napoleon was appointed artillery commander of the French forces besieging Toulon, where royalists with the aid of the British had risen against the revolutionaries. Using a cunning plan of his own devising, Napoleon forced the British ships to flee and the town was retaken. The following year, he devised another cunning plan to put down a royalist revolt in Paris, clearing the streets, as he once famously remarked, with a 'whiff of grapeshot' from cannons he had brazenly captured from the rebels. His audacious feats brought him fame, money and the favour of the ruling directorate; it also brought him his wife, Josephine de Beauharnais (creator of the less well-known Beauharnais sauce) whom he married on 9 March 1796.

Less than three weeks later, secretly delighted by the success of his cunning plans and keen to try a few more, he said 'Not tonight Josephine' and went off to invade Italy. Having done that, he defeated the Papal States, invaded Austria and ended a thousand years of Venetian independence by conquering the city of canals during peak tourist season. Heady days for *le petit caporal*, the somewhat inaccurate soubriquet given him by his adoring troops, because he was a general, not a corporal, and he was not by the standards of the time particularly short. It was intended more as a term of endearment, although the love didn't extend to the conservative wing of the French political establishment, who were growing increasingly alarmed by his influence. So he swiftly organised a coup d'état to purge the remaining royalists and returned to Paris triumphant.

Quickly growing bored despite the best efforts of Josephine, he suggested an invasion of Egypt and within weeks was off across the Mediterranean to liberate the Musselman from their Ottoman oppressors. Things went relatively well on land but at sea the French were all at sea, suffering a heavy defeat at the hands—well, hand—of Horatio Nelson. Meanwhile, at home, things weren't looking too good on the political front so Napoleon nipped back to Paris for another quick coup d'état and appointed himself First Consul, reforming the administrative system, fixing the roads and sewers, overhauling taxation and introducing a new code of civil law, named in all modesty the Napoleonic Code.

Having done all that, in 1800 Napoleon scooted back to Italy, which the Austrians had re-invaded while he was invading Egypt. He eventually routed them and sued for peace, although the European monarchs were wary of recognising a republic such as France and were forever organising coalitions against the Corsican upstart. Britain was proving an eternal thorn in his side so to defend French territorial interests in North America, Napoleon sent an army to reconquer Haiti. Sadly, yellow fever got the better of them and, realising he couldn't hold on to the American land possessions, he sold them to the United States in the Louisiana Purchase for a lousy three cents an acre.

Despite his poor real-estate credentials, Napoleon had himself crowned emperor in December 1804. Within months, Britain had joined the Third Coalition against the French expansionist and his plans for an invasion of England were put on hold after Nelson's stunning victory at Trafalgar. Within months, the Austrians and the Russians were preparing to invade France, forcing Napoleon to crush them at the battle of Austerlitz in December 1805. He then went on to invade Prussia, Poland and the German states, handing them over to various friends and family members to rule on France's behalf. His invasion of Spain and Portugal in 1807 didn't go quite so well, his army suffering huge losses and battling a protracted guerrilla war until 1814.

In 1810, Napoleon remarried. Despite their eternal love for each other, he and Josephine had been unable to produce an heir, so Josephine had agreed to a divorce, conveniently the first under the newly introduced Napoleonic Code. Given his fondness for invading and crushing Austria, it was odd that Napoleon married an Austrian, the Archduchess Marie Louise, who presented him with an heir, Napoleon Francis Joseph Charles, or Napoleon Jnr, as he was known to avoid confusion. Sadly he died at the age of twenty-one, virtually a prisoner of his Austrian grandparents, unable to fulfil his father's vision of a glorified French empire.

Domestic problems aside, Napoleon's biggest mistake was his less-than-cunning plan to invade Russia. In June 1812, he led the *Grande Armée* of 650,000 men across the border. The Russians avoided direct confrontation, preferring instead to retreat and burn everything as they went, thus drawing the French into the barren and increasingly cold heartland. Disease, desertion and constant skirmishing whittled away their numbers and when, in late September, Napoleon finally entered Moscow (which the Russians had burned anyway, so there were no shops open) it was a pyrrhic victory at best and the French were forced into bitter retreat scarcely a month later. A mere 40,000 Frenchmen escaped Russia with their lives. Only half that number still had their backpacks.

By now, almost every European nation had joined in an alliance against Napoleon. Sweden joined in late 1813, and the addition of their flat-pack furniture skills proved the final straw; Paris was occupied in March 1814. Napoleon abdicated and was imprisoned on the island of Elba as Louis XVIII was restored to power. But that was not the end—Napoleon had one final cunning plan. He escaped and returned to the French mainland to re-assume the mantle of Emperor. Riding alone to confront the 5th Regiment sent to capture him, he dismounted from his horse and said 'Soldiers of the Fifth, you recognise me. If any man would shoot his emperor, you may do so now.' Luckily, no one did and with the traditional French love of the grand but futile gesture, they hoisted him aloft with many 'Huzzahs!' and bore him to Paris, where he ruled for a hundred days before the final crushing defeat at the hands of the Duke of Wellington at the Battle of Waterloo in June 1815.

Caught fleeing to the United States, Napoleon was exiled to St Helena and died there six years later. The cause of his death has been widely disputed. The original autopsy blamed stomach cancer, although some historians suspected he had been poisoned by arsenic—a lock of his hair contained arsenic levels at least thirty times higher than normal. This theory has since been discounted and the arsenic levels blamed on hair tonic or syphilis treatment, arsenic being popular at the time in both medications. It was even commonly found in wallpaper. Judging from the evidence to date, stomach cancer seems the most likely; it was, after all, the disease that killed his father.

Napoleon's legacy continues to this day. His legal code still forms the basis of French jurisprudence and his tactics are studied in military academies the world over. He changed the course of warfare, introducing the conscription army and the concept of total war; victory was now decided by the complete destruction of the enemy and the capitulation of the whole state. He exported the anti-feudal ideas of the Revolution and the Age of Enlightenment, expanding the boundaries of scientific knowledge and briefly cementing French influence in European affairs. Critics counter that he was vainglorious and reckless, costing the lives of millions of Frenchmen for little gain, bankrupting the nation and setting a precedent for autocrats and tyrants for centuries to come. In the end, what was the point of seventeen years of continuous warfare? France had slipped to the rank of a secondary power, was even more detested in Europe and the monarchy made a comeback after all the gains of the Revolution. If only Napoleon had known when to stop ...

## 262  Never knowing when enough is enough

Napoleon's biggest problem was that he never knew when to quit while he was ahead. No sooner had he invaded one country than he was off crushing another. His armies were constantly over-extended; instead of concentrating on consolidating his gains, he'd launch into another grandiose enterprise. Invading Russia was typical; access to unlimited vodka aside, what did he realistically stand to gain for the expenditure of such enormous effort? He embodied the imperial ambitions of the nineteenth century, an insatiable belief that expansion equals growth which finds its modern equivalent in the cut-throat world of the corporate takeover, although these days people are usually retrenched rather than left to rot in the frozen wastes of Poland.

## 263  Using an arsenic-based hair tonic

Sure, you might get the immediate results you're after but what about the long-term side effects? It makes sense that you don't want fly-away split ends when you're invading Austria for the umpteenth time but these things can come back to haunt you. A non-toxic gel can quite as easily give you the 'just been to the salon' look you want for any military campaign and offers a confident hold in windy Alpine conditions.

## 264 Not calculating the odds

Napoleon was a brilliant tactician and no slouch as a mathematician—he has a theorem named after him—but his blinding faith in his own abilities led him to make unreasonable assumptions. There comes a time when you must acknowledge that the weight of numbers is against you. Never forget the big picture. Unfortunately, for the millions of Europeans he sent to their untimely deaths, defeat was not in Napoleon's vocabulary. Neither were 'antidisestablishmentarianism', 'radar' or 'penicillin'.

## 265 Never accepting compromise

Even when offered peace settlements that would have left France with greater landmass and power than ever before, Napoleon refused to compromise and demanded total surrender. Not only did this make him unpopular, it also turned him into a tyrant. On retreat in Egypt, he killed the prisoners and the sick in order to hasten the march. He reintroduced slavery into France and was prepared to sacrifice any number of soldiers—even his own—to achieve his goals. The names Stalin and Hitler spring to mind, although their legacy on sewerage systems and the penal code is not as good.

## 266 Involving your family in the business

This might work well in a fruit shop but in the administration of the conquered Papal States and other parts of the Empire it's not world's best practice. Napoleon kept it all in the family with some very mixed results—he made his brother Louis king of Holland then dethroned him for becoming too Dutch. (Louis's son Charles later became Napoleon III, the last emperor of France.) His sister Caroline was made queen of Naples, even though she later betrayed him; while another brother Jérôme was anointed king of the short-lived state of Westphalia. And here's a funny thing: in 1908 Jérôme's grandson, Charles Joseph Bonaparte, founded the US Bureau of Investigation (BOI), which became the FBI. Small world, isn't it?

# 14
# THE HOME HANDYPERSON

'The most important work you and I will ever do will be within the walls of our own homes.'
*Harold B Lee*

This page may be used as a To Do list. Alternatively, you may write on it.

I don't think he's referring to putting up that extra set of shelves in the laundry, but for the home handyperson, there is nothing more important than the challenges they face in the ceaseless quest for home improvement. This is where the ineffective take centre stage, fuelling a growth industry for tradesmen who are kept busy repairing the damage done by the do-it-yourself enthusiasts. People are professional for a reason—they know what they're doing. It is the extraordinary presumption of the home handyperson that keeps the shelves of hardware stores groaning with product—two out of every three things they cheerfully sell turn out to be the wrong size, model, application or colour.

In the past, home improvement was largely a male domain. A woman's role was to outline the vision; the man was assigned to fail to fulfil it. Now, thanks to lightweight materials, cheap power tools and the inexorable rise of flat-pack furniture, women are equally capable of ruining everything they touch.

## 267 Thinking that chipboard is water resistant

## 268 Assuming there's only one type of sand

## 269 Regarding the manufacturer's recommendations as a conspiracy theory

Manufacturers, as a rule, provide instructions and recommendations for their products that are borne of years of research and testing. You, on the other hand, come to a hardware product with relative naïvety. This is probably the first time you've installed a toilet seat; at best, you've done it once or twice before. So, if they recommend that you fit a rubber washer on either side of the retaining bolt, it's a good idea to replace the two rubber washers that accidentally rolled down the drain before proceeding with the installation. Likewise, as you go to hang the gilt mirror you picked up at the markets, if the hook has a recommended top load of 6 kilos, don't automatically assume it's all a con and they're only saying that to make you buy two hooks.

## 270 Optimistically believing that near enough is good enough

It might have fuelled the career of A Flock of Seagulls, but in the world of DIY, near enough is never good enough. Two millimetres off plumb at the base of your brick garden wall means 80 millimetres out by the top. That means your lattice inserts won't fit, no matter how hard you thump them with a mallet, and your decorative finials will topple off in the first light breeze. And while you may be able to convince *yourself* that near enough is good enough, it will most certainly not be for your significant other. *You* might only be able to see that rough patch on a painted wall when the light hits it at a certain angle but they'll be able to see it in the dark.

## 271 Not 'measuring twice, cutting once'

## 272 Not being able to read a spirit level or refusing to believe it if you can

This is where the rot sets in. The construction game, be it a skyscraper or said set of shelves in the laundry, is all about angles and accurate measurement. If the bubble's not smack bang in the middle of the spirit level, no amount of wishful thinking is going to change it. Start again.

## 273 Not having the right tools for the job

## 274 Forgetting that drill bits, blades and saws need sharpening

## 275 Failing to allow for 15 per cent wastage

## 276 Mistaking quantity for quality

They sell tiles at $6 a square metre for a very good reason: they're crap.

## 277 Underestimating the weight borne by any shelf

Usually done for two reasons: incompetence and reluctance to pay for the more expensive, load appropriate brackets. Shelving is a deceptively tricky area of home improvement, involving as it does measurement, levelling, wall fixtures, spacing and planning. Each is a recipe for disaster in its own right. There are at least thirty ways to attach a bracket to a wall, depending on the structural material involved. The number of spring-loaded toggles, grips, plugs and fasteners that can be put into plasterboard alone is mind-boggling, and the only thing they have in common is that the hole they leave in the wall will be bigger than the hole you began with. Remember to calculate your maximum load potential—no point experimenting with empty boxes if they're all going to be full of ball bearings on the day. Are small children going to be tempted to swing on it? Will domestic animals choose to sleep on it?

Here's a tip for a job well done: pay a professional to do it.

## 278 Attempting any job that requires a ladder more than your height

## 279 Using a router without instruction

## 280 Believing a screw is a curly nail

## 281 Saying 'It can't be that difficult.'

This is a simple admission that in fact it is. Thankfully, most home handypersons have an innate sense of self-preservation and are understandably reluctant to tackle the jobs that pose a threat to life, like electrical work or painting a high-pitched roof. They often delegate those duties to a mate with dubious certification from TAFE who can do it on the cheap. But occasionally the ineffective, having little sense of their own limitations, will attempt the impossible, until they reach that awful moment of mistaking the red wire for the green one and are last seen being hurled against the newly installed kitchen shelves in a blinding flash of light.

## 282 Believing the rubber-soled sandal is protective footwear

## 283 Thinking it won't take long to paint these two rooms

One benign area where we all think we can make a difference and save a bit of cash is house painting, harbouring as we do fond memories of our youths when we'd grab a tin of paint and spruce up the rented place we were occupying, adding a few shelves from planks of wood on house bricks and knocking together a granite kitchen with ceramic splashbacks and terrazzo floor out of old bits and pieces we found on the vacant lot down the road.

Think again: there are any number of ways you can do a bad job with a brush in your hand.

## 284 Selecting a colour scheme without consulting your partner

## 285 Failing to prepare surfaces

Like every job about the home, it all begins with the preparation: you cannot build success on a poor foundation. If you don't put masking tape on the windows, you're going to paint the glass, no matter how careful you are, then spend the next ten years saying 'I must get a razor blade onto those windows.' If you don't put drop sheets down, you're going to spray the floor with a fine rain of matte finish Tropical Sunrise, no matter how careful you are. If you don't kill the mould before you put the paint over it, you're going to end up with a wall the texture of porridge. These are not maybes, they're givens.

**286 Saying 'I can sand that bit back later'**

**287 Thinning paint to make it go further**

**288 Leaving brushes in a jam jar of turpentine for a week**

**289 Not allowing adequate drying time**

Too often, in the desire to admire the finished handiwork, the masking tape along the skirting board (assuming you've put it on) is ripped off prematurely, taking a ragged edge of gloss paint with it. Then, in a fit of pique, the tape is scrunched into a ball which sticks to your foot and drags gloss off-white all over the carpet.

**290 Edging by hand**

**291 Unrealistic expectations of the power of No More Gaps**

**292 Painting a ceiling without wearing a shower cap**

**293 Pretending it was the previous owner's handiwork when you hire a painter to salvage the disaster**

To which he'll tut-tut and say, 'And didn't they make a fine old mess of it?', even though you know he can smell the fresh paint and your hair is still so spattered with flat ceiling white it looks like the pepper-and-flour mixture for crumbing cutlets.

# A Day in the Life of an Ineffective

Monday 1 March

Having finally decided to implement New Year's resolutions, set alarm for early morning power walk at 6.30 a.m. Eventually get out of bed at 7.50 a.m. and hit the shower—literally hit it because of unrepaired faulty tap that now requires brute force. Compact remaining soap slivers into bar even smaller than the ones they have in motels—must add soap to shopping list which was on handy fridge magnet but has now disappeared. Towel not only as stiff as an ironing board (try to conjure up distant memory of ironing board for appropriate analogous comparison) but smells like a leaking car boot due to failure to wash with last month's sheets. Or was that the month before? Must check brittleness of bed sheets to determine.

Underpants worth risking for another day but unable to find matching pair of black socks. Gingerly recover two from laundry basket, rinse with lavender hand wash then microwave for express dry. Kitchen now smells like a tourist shop in historic Hahndorf and sock elastic has vulcanised. Hold up with two rubber bands but begin to lose blood circulation to feet. Socks continue to heat while wearing so left heel suffers second degree burn. Abandon closed footwear and decide to instigate Crazy Thongs Day at work instead.

Weetbix box contains one bix and two tennis star swap cards, both Wayne Arthurs. Consume dry, due to milk being four days past expiry—just as well, there being no clean bowls anyway due to failure to begin dishwasher cycle before retiring. Also need to add dishwashing powder to missing list. Home-made marmalade appears to have the consistency of orange water before realising I've opened refrigerated pathology sample by mistake. That means the laboratory is currently testing mid-stream marmalade which may skew the results. Write on hand: Ring doctor re: sample. Can't find doctor's number—was on another handy fridge magnet along with emergency gas service and local real-estate agent contact details but now gone. Remember using same to stop window rattling but no longer in window either. Check under leg of wobbly dining chair with no luck. Try to find Yellow Pages but remember throwing it away in misconceived attempt to go paperless when internet broadband was installed. Try going online but ISP not responding. Ring help desk. Put on hold but reassured that call is important to them.

Half hour later, try to reassemble phone after thrashing it against computer. Eventually abandon repair job as hopeless and realise that plan to catch bus has now gone out window due to lateness of hour. Will have to take car again instead. Hunt for coins for parking meter—resort to Tooth Fairy money allocated for godchild, make note to replace. Realise two dollars will only buy eighteen minutes of parking so revert to original bus plan.

No rides left on multiple bus ticket so surrender inadequate Tooth Fairy money to rude driver who makes me get off four stops before work. Right thong breaks at repair point; Tarzan's Grip not what it used to be. Arrive at work to find no one has missed me except man from accounts who does the footy tipping. Can never remember his name—same goes for me with most people in organisation. Have tried mental labels, word association, picturing colleagues in nude, etc.

but nothing seems to stick except frightening mental images. Equally pointless entering footy tipping competition; now have enough wooden spoons to open shop.

Attempt to bind last quarter's sales results, having spent best part of morning getting computer connected to network printer. Pretended to man from IT that someone else had put that cable in that slot but now may have to call maintenance because binder has just taken the bottom three centimetres of my tie clean off. Not good look for sales meeting, especially combined with Crazy Thongs. Work experience girl effortlessly fixes binder and collates my documents; obviously they're still teaching something in the schools.

Low blood-sugar attack at 11 a.m., due to inadequate breakfast. Binge-eat Tim Tams (pretend I'm Chinese and can't read post-it note on packet reading: 'Keep off—these are for 6th floor only!') before realising I have just eaten Weight Watchers quota for three days. Resolve to have skim milk in coffee and salad sandwich for lunch.

Resolve withers on vine as enter Hungry Jack's for Double Whopper with cheese—downsize fries in fit of guilt. Small strawberry shake, some of which ends up down shirt front when trying to get the last bits out with a straw. Worsen stain by rubbing it with an ice cube from dispensing machine. Spot work experience girl in pub having a drink with the large-framed girl from reception. Unable to resolve moral dilemma as to whether I should tell the boss, tell her parents or join them for a stiff one. Guilty mental chuckle at sexist double entendre.

Afternoon passes slowly. Discover website of time-lapsed photos of celebrity backsides; you then have to match them to owners' faces, crazy stuff. Forward link to everyone in address book, they'll get a good laugh. During indoor cricket game in the corridor accidentally break large-framed girl's glasses playing a lofted cover drive—no wonder they didn't want me to bat. Her black eye will hopefully heal before she's matron of honour at her sister's wedding on Saturday. Sales meeting going quite well until discovery that document is bound in reverse order—I panic and blame work experience girl then tell boss that she was in the pub at lunchtime with large-framed girl—no wonder she copped that ball in the face, reaction times slowed etc. Feel guilty.

Sub committee of social committee set up to investigate Crazy Thongs Day as annual activity. Have to determine which charity should benefit. Colleague suggests World Sex Aids Day, gets a small laugh but I don't reveal it's not his, he read it on the internet. Find out it was my turn to do the office Lotto last week. Pray to God our numbers don't come up because I forgot to put them in. Remember using money for taxi after car locked in parking station overnight. Make quick mental inventory of assets I could sell to cover the debt if we won. Hopeless—will have to kill myself.

Google 'painless suicide' and find gross site on dead bodies. Consider forwarding link to everyone in address book, but have doubts they'll get a good laugh. Fudge timesheet at sign-off to cover late arrival and ask work experience girl if she fancies a drink after work. She says she has a doctor's appointment which I try to believe. Attempt to get money out of ATM which swallows card after third wrong guess at PIN. I'm sure that number is mother's birthday. Swallow pride and ask the large-framed girl for a loan at the bus stop then go to meet friends at Thai restaurant. Sit there for half an hour before realising it's the wrong restaurant. Battery expires on mobile phone while ringing friend but eventually track them down in Indian place just as they're asking for the bill.

Decide to kick on but then the only two people I actually like change their minds and go home, so left with losers from storeroom and strange girl who reads auras. Discover I have negative energy and should drink St Johns Wort tea. Try to think of witty comeback about warts but fail, make feeble tea-based joke instead. Think of good one ten minutes later in men's room but accidentally splash trousers at sink, now everyone will think I failed to shake adequately. Try to angle hand dryer onto crotch—get odd look from bloke coming in.

Come out to find losers and strange girl have gone. Excellent, didn't have to borrow money to buy a round. Get home to find someone has forced open letterbox with a screwdriver. Remember that was me after losing letterbox key and discovering spare key had gone to God on handy fridge magnet. Third reminder for overdue electricity bill—hard to read because lights have all gone out. Rue not placing emergency torch under kitchen sink. Light aromatherapy candle given as Valentine's Day gift by ex-girlfriend. Scent reminds me again of girlfriend before her; realise it was bad romantic move to tell ex-girlfriend same just after receipt of gift.

In semi-darkness, mistakenly brush teeth with toothbrush reserved for cleaning grout. One day. Try to set alarm clock for 6.30 power walk before realising clock runs on disconnected mains power. Resolve to become more effective as human being before falling into fitful sleep. Having neglected to extinguish aromatherapy candle, awake to fire brigade putting axe through door, etc. and so on.

# 15
# THE PARENT CRAP

'They fuck you up, your mum and dad.
They may not mean to, but they do.'
*Philip Larkin*

This page may be used for craft activities.

All of us—clones aside—have had a parent at some stage in our lives. Most of us have at some stage suffered, in varying degrees, under their ineffective parenting. Those of us who have children of our own are now perfectly placed to repeat the same mistakes. Parenthood presents the less capable with endless opportunities for failure—if you can't manage your own life, think of the inherent dangers of trying to manage someone else's. If you're planning a family of your own, this chapter, like all the realities of parenthood, is probably best avoided. If you have remained childless and are perfectly happy with the situation, you may read and gloat.

## 294 Having children

Yes, I know how marvellous the miracles of creation are and what joy they bring, but if anything is going to ruin your life it's the pitter-patter of tiny feet. As I watch gay friends swan cheerfully about the world without the need of extended childcare, I can only bitterly think: 'Oh yes, it's all right for you with your disposable income and a social life but someone's got to go to all the trouble of making poofs. And this is all the thanks we get?'

If you're ineffective to begin with, having children will only exponentially exacerbate your problem. If you think you're hopelessly messy, wait until you see a toddler with a black Texta and a chocolate ice-cream in a room full of Scandinavian furniture. If you have no idea of how to keep a wardrobe organised, you're an expert compared with any seven year old. The sheer relentlessness of parenting cannot be anticipated or prepared for; unless you're willing to lock your children in the car in a casino car park with a packet of chips and a portable DVD player, there is no respite.

### 295 Having a birth plan

Ante-natal classes are primarily designed to lull you into a false sense of security, giving you the naïve impression that childbirth can be a pleasant experience. Fathers often quote the birth of their children as the most awe-inspiring experience of their lives but that's usually because they're not the ones with ten stitches in their genitals. Massage oils, favourite calming music selections and therapeutic backrubs all go straight out the window when the first serious contraction kicks in. If you must have a birth plan, ensure that it only details the amount and timing of pain-relieving drugs. And please, no photos. No one, outside certain specialist websites, wants to see your slide-show or DVD of life's first magical moments.

### 296 Playing Mozart to your unborn child

It can't hear it! And even if it could, it would have no knowledge of it because the brain has not yet developed to the stage of recording memory. Can you remember anything before the age of six without having a photo to look at? Far better to play Britney Spears to your child as it labours down the birth canal in the slim hope of some sort of Pavlovian connection to an unpleasant experience when it's confronted with such ghastly music later in life.

Similarly, avoid the modern obsession with flash cards, baby proms and accelerated infant learning. What's the rush? We are robbing our children of childhood. Why should a kindergarten child be able to discuss Shakespeare? Be happy if they can walk in a straight line and skip after a fashion. Keep them away from computers, no matter how important you think so-called computer literacy to be. Modern computers are so easy to use, a child can do it. Where's the challenge in click-and-drag colouring in? Get them started on the hard stuff like pencil and paper or Play-Doh. Anyone who can make a half-decent dinosaur out of plasticine deserves a medal.

### 297 Allowing sugar to be introduced into the diet

Be wary of well-meaning elderly relatives who say 'One little sweety won't do them any harm' as they wave a jelly bean in front of your mesmerised infant. It might not choke them but it will have a devastating effect on your life from that point on. Their first word will be 'Confectionery!', repeated like Chinese water torture every time you stray within two hundred metres of a shop.

### 298 Forgetting that for a child the magic word is 'NOW'

### 299 Saying 'All right, you can have just one.'

Any moment of weakness is seized upon by children with the zeal of a lioness bringing down a hapless wildebeest. In their universe, boundaries only exist to be pushed to the limit; rules are only there to be broken after a softening-up period of extended whinging and nagging. Marketers recognise this, having identified the 'nag-factor' in any sales opportunity and cunningly positioning chocolate at the eye level of a small child making their parent's life misery in the check-out queue. Advertisers positively encourage extreme emotions in junior shoppers, knowing full-well that only the iron-willed or profoundly deaf can withstand a tantrum thrown with all stops out.

## 300 Introducing television as a recreational pastime

The electronic babysitter, so enthusiastically resorted to by harried parents for a moment's peace when they return from the supermarket, quickly becomes the digital tyrant. Studies have shown even moderate amounts of television viewing can have a deleterious effect on your child. Fairly obvious conclusion, the cynical might think, witnessing what it does to adults who are old enough to know better. Occasionally, proponents with degrees in media studies will counter with arguments that the complicated plot structures of *Bananas in Pyjamas* encourage lateral thinking and problem solving but is it likely your children will ever be confronted with the need to find Morgan the Teddy Bear's slippers in a real life scenario? Once switched on, television becomes ever more difficult to switch off. Elaborate rationing systems involving charts, stars and unspecified consequences do little. The threat to remove it altogether rings hollow because the children know that you'll be glued to it, stiff drink in hand, as soon as they've gone to bed.

## 301 Encouraging craft sessions

Craft works brilliantly on *Play School* simply because there are no children present at the time. When you attempt to replicate the process at home, it quickly descends into a paste-sodden free-for-all that ends with the children inhaling glitter and your misshapen cardboard efforts bearing no resemblance at all to the planets in the solar system or whatever they were meant to represent. By all means attempt craft in a plastic lined room with adequate drainage; otherwise leave well alone until the children are old enough to get work as *Play School* presenters where craft may be of some practical use.

## 302 Suggesting a themed birthday party

Children's parties have become a growth industry, just like everything else that is largely pointless and was once more than adequately handled by amateurs. In nine out of ten OECD countries, the juvenile party industry employs more people than shipbuilding and will soon overtake the aerospace industry in terms of GDP. Parties have become status symbols—for the parents, of course, not the children—and almost anything is available for hire: bouncy castles, chateaux de bounce, fairies, clowns, petting zoos, reptile displays, action heroes, kids' bands, magicians, junior crack-house rappers or face painters guaranteed allergy-free. Don't even think about it: all you'll get is an enormous bill and a world-weary 'Is that it?' from birthday boy or girl.

## 303 Thinking you can be your child's best friend

You can't—you're their parent. Hopefully, you'll like them and they'll like you in return. But from a child's point of view, the emotional attachment to a parent generally follows a parabolic shape: intense to begin with, then diminishing, gradually increasing again before rapidly growing as they realise you're about to render them an orphan. A good friend can be non-judgemental; try as hard as they might, parents find it almost impossible to be so. Nor should they be. Their role is essentially to civilise the untamed (though admittedly small and relatively helpless) barbarian that is entrusted to their care. Hard decisions have to be made, even if they'll ultimately be ignored. A whole lifetime of emotional baggage and neuroses have to be handed on to the next generation. (And let me tell you, you ungrateful wretch, it's a very good friend indeed who'll wipe your backside or clean up your vomit at three in the morning!)

## 304 Making quality time for your children

The comedian Barry Humphries once observed: 'Quality time is time you'd rather spend doing something else.' If you feel a need to make quality time, it's probably too late. The best thing you can give a child in its early years is time on their terms. (Difficult, because one can pretend to be Harry Potter's horrid cousin Dudley only so many times before insanity beckons.) But quality time is immediately compromised by the burden of obligation, like the dreaded family outing that is deemed essential to building domestic relationships but will only end in bitter fighting and sobs of anguish—and that's just from the parents.

Quality time is part and parcel of that other awful catch-phrase of the early twenty-first century: work/life balance.

This implies that 'life' is something that is only carried out on a casual basis and its hours can be allocated: 'I'll start life at 5.30 p.m. and knock off at 8 a.m. the next morning.' What a damning indictment of modern society, that work has become something devoid of life, that we have allowed the Machine to dominate us to the point where we now work longer hours to earn the money to pay consultants and buy self-help books to tell us how to not work so much. It's like working overtime to earn the money to send your kids to private schools—why don't you just go home early and teach them something yourself? Surely you know something worth passing on to the next generation. Or save up and take them around the world—it's probably cheaper.

I have a sneaking suspicion that many people, despite their protestations, work longer hours simply to avoid being with their children. Parenting, especially in the early years, is the hardest job you will ever be called upon to do—leaving the house to go to work can seem like a holiday.

## 305 Living vicariously through your children

Don't try to make your child everything you wanted to be. Thanks to the human genome, they're going to largely turn into what you are, not what you could or should have been. Of course we all deny that we essentially become our parents, but that's what keeps human nature so consistent through the generations. The best thing you can do for your child, short of having them adopted out, is to lead by positive example. If you lead a fulfilling life, they'll flourish in the environment it creates.

## 306 Forgetting that children are not made of glass

There is a growing tendency to try to wrap children in cotton wool, to insulate them from every potential danger or unpleasantness. Motivated by our own increasing fears, we try to protect our offspring from finding things out the hard way, be it falling off a scooter at speed or discovering that not everyone shares their parents' high opinion of their creative talents. All this does is stifle the child's resilience—the ability to bounce back from setbacks is the most important skill you can teach them; seeking to avoid unpleasant realities altogether is counter-productive. I'm not suggesting you introduce them to known pederasts but perhaps you could drop them from small shrubs or brutally and honestly appraise their jazz ballet skills—it'll all help in the long run.

## 307 Forgetting that a child's self-esteem has to be earned

There is no point in continuously reinforcing a child's supposed self-esteem in the face of all evidence to the contrary. The modern fashion of presenting a medal to every child in a running race is ridiculous. By all means award a house point for having a go but children aren't stupid—if they come dead last, they know they can't run as fast as the others and recognise that, having volunteered to enter an arbitrary test of athletic meritocracy, all hollow spoils to the victor and hail the magnificent also-rans! That's certainly how I saw it from several hundred metres behind the pack, knowing, between gasps, that I'd have to find some other field of enterprise in which to shine. We can't all be good at everything; to pretend otherwise is deceitful. True self-esteem comes from recognising our own strengths, but an unfortunate yet inescapable part of that process is recognising and accepting our weaknesses.

Take comfort in the words of Walt Whitman: 'Have you heard that it was good to gain the day? I also say it is good to fall, battles are lost in the same spirit in which they are won.'

## 308 Feeling guilty if you don't like your children

If it's as in not liking *at all*, there may be a problem, but the occasional burst of intense dislike for your offspring is perfectly normal. At least I hope it is. Don't forget they're always at their best when they're asleep, a perfect time to recharge the batteries of your emotional bonding.

## 309 Feeling guilty if your children don't eat vegetables

Remember: don't feel guilty if you haven't done anything wrong. As long as you've made an effort to force capsicum down your children's throats at some point in their lives, rest easy. Most kids would rather not eat vegetables—I know a family where tomato sauce is considered a vegetable—but the palate matures with age and they may begin to accept the pickle on the quarter pounder with cheese and discover that not all fluids have to be carbonated. If the child is upright, alert and capable of movement, your nutritional efforts are probably adequate for this stage in life.

## 310 Sacrificing your own happiness for the sake of your children

It is paradoxical that parents struggle to make the next generation live better lives than they had, then bang on about how much better things were when they were kids. It is natural to want the best for your children but to do so at the expense of your own happiness is counter-productive. By all means make sacrifices to ensure their education and physical wellbeing—give them a kidney if they need it—but a happy parent offers a child the best chance of a happy childhood. Look at the parents in Enid Blyton's *Famous Five*—they were always jolly, largely because they were saying goodbye to the kids as they headed off for five weeks' summer hols at Thistledown Farm.

## ROLE MODELS FOR THE INEFFECTIVE

*Number 7*

GERALD RATNER was born in London in 1949 into a family of jewellery traders, joining the family business in 1966. Having observed, in the Petticoat Lane markets as a boy, that 'the stallholders who shouted the loudest and appeared to give the best offers sold the most', Ratner applied the same philosophy to his jewellery stores, selling a low- price range of goods and offering amazing discounts advertised on bright, fluorescent posters.

It was a strategy that worked: from 130 stores with an annual profit of £13 million, by 1990 Ratner had built his retail empire up to 2500 stores with 25,000 employees and an annual turnover of £1.2 billion. In the heady, greed-is-good days of the 1980s, Ratner was an entrepreneurial star, so in April 1991, the Institute of Directors invited him to address 7000 of his fellow businessmen in the Albert Hall.

Sharing the secrets of his success, Ratner made the following career-shattering observations: 'We also do cut-glass sherry decanters complete with six glasses on a silver-plated tray that your butler can serve you drinks on, all for £4.95. People say, "How can you sell this for such a low price?" I say, "Because it's total crap."' He later went on to admit that some of the earrings his company sold were 'cheaper than a Marks and Spencer prawn sandwich but probably wouldn't last as long'.

Unbeknownst to Ratner, the Institute of Directors had sent an advance copy of his speech to the *Daily Mirror* and, sniffing a story, they'd sent a reporter along. These were the days when the recession was starting to bite and there was a public backlash against the flashy high-flyers. The *Daily Mirror* splashed the quote across its front page the next day. Rival tabloid *The Sun* joined the media frenzy and Ratner quickly became a laughing stock.

Within weeks, £500 million was wiped from the company's value as angry customers demanded either their money back or an exchange for a prawn sandwich. Ratner hung on for eighteen months but was eventually sacked from his own company, which expunged the family name and re-branded itself as the Signet Group. His humiliation was swift and total—for the next seven years, by his own admission, he sat on a couch watching daytime television.

Ironically, Ratner had used similar jokes in corporate speeches for years and in his defence claimed that he never meant to offend his customers, nor did he know that the speech was on the public record. It's possible that he was ambushed by rivals in the IOD who ensured the press would be at the meeting but he ignored the cardinal rule of salesmanship: never tell the truth about your product. Even more ironically, Ratner has relaunched his jewellery business online and is now in demand once again as a corporate speaker advising on how to succeed in business!

The true horror of this story, of course, is that there are people walking the streets who don't realise that six cut-glasses on a silver-plated tray with decanter that sell for £4.95

cannot be anything but total crap. Heaven forbid, for world commerce, that they ever do.

### 311 Not knowing who your audience is

### 117 Bad timing of moments of hollow triumphalism (see above: bank managers)

Ratner assumed that his audience shared his patronising attitude to the naïve customers who bought his products. Undoubtedly most of them did, all except for one little cub reporter who suddenly knew what was causing her pierced ears to swell up like balloons.

### 312 Thinking that honesty without tact is always the best policy

There are times when it's better not to tell the truth. That is not to say you should lie; simply refrain from revealing the self-evident. The oaf who spills your drink in the pub may indeed be uglier than you but if he's bigger, it's inadvisable to tell him so. George Washington, when he told his father that he had chopped down the cherry tree, knew he was on fairly safe ground and confident that his honesty would be rewarded. Had he confessed to a homicidal cherry-tree enthusiast, things could've turned out quite differently.

### 313 Wanting to make a fortune by selling total crap

Ratner is not alone in this—the Chinese economic miracle is kept alive by the world's insatiable appetite for total crap. Ratner now sources his jewellery from India, the next great manufacturing powerhouse for cheap not-entirely-durable consumer goods. The shameless exploitation of the poor materialists (see above on the psychology of consumerism) has been with us since the apes first straightened then opened a shop, but every now and then karma steps in and knocks the shysters from grace.

# 16
# IGNORING HISTORY

'Those who ignore history are doomed to repeat it.'
*A fact*

This page may be used to recommend this book as a gift suggestion.

Like the genetic inheritance we all carry inside ourselves, there are patterns of behaviour in the affairs of mankind that repeat themselves ad nauseam. We forget that the present is shaped by the past and not by the future. Only by studying the patterns of history can we avoid the mistakes that befell those who have gone before us, like shoulder pads, extremely wide belts and the musical stylings of The Brotherhood of Man. Look at Hitler—motoring along quite nicely, all poised to conquer Britain, until he decides to invade Russia instead, completely forgetting that Napoleon had tried the very same thing just over a hundred years before with very ordinary results. (See Role Models for the Ineffective: Number 6.) Not only that, having launched the Wermacht eastwards, he repeats the same mistakes that the wily Corsican made all those years ago: overstretched supply lines, inadequate winter provisions, insufficient troop numbers and a belief in his own abilities that bore little or no relation to reality. Result: total defeat, 22 million dead and not even the *1812 Overture* to show for it.

Have you ever thought about invading a country with a land mass greater than Africa but a lot colder and a population that will never surrender, even when they're dead? Well, think again.

### 314 Invading Russia

### 315 Thinking 'Things will be different this time round'

They won't be, unless you make them different. The flipside of ignoring history is a blind faith in the benevolence of the future. Call it fate, call it kismet or even *que sera sera* but resignation to an as-yet-unseen outcome can be counterproductive. True, there are some things beyond your ability to change but there is only one absolute certainty in life and that is death. (Taxes you can avoid by not earning enough or assuming an elaborate secret identity and living on berries in the forest.) Anything else is still up for grabs and what you actively do will have a bearing, however small, on the result. A butterfly flaps its wings in the Amazon, and lo, your shower rail comes away from the wall at precisely the same moment that the hot water runs out. It's all cause and effect. The first step in escaping a vicious circle is recognising it for what it is and then moving away tangentially.

### 316 Believing that lightning doesn't strike twice

### 317 Pooh-poohing a rise in the Southern Oscillation Index

### 318 Forgetting that what goes up comes down

Not everything you learned at school is completely useless. Newton's law of gravity is just one of a million inescapable truths that cannot be altered. Ah, you say, but what about space travel? What about escaping the pull of earth's gravity through rocket propulsion? Can we not escape the predetermined through wilful enterprise? Well, yes, but only to a point; sooner or later you will come under the gravitational pull of some other heavenly body and plummet to a fiery end. Icarus flew too close to the sun and his waxen wings melted to nothing. Try it yourself and you'll quickly discover that waxen wings won't even help you down off the garage roof. Temporarily escaping or avoiding historical reality will only end with a sudden and brutal re-acquaintance.

## 319 Introducing the cane toad

In the mid-twentieth century, Australia introduced the cane toad from South America as a biological control against an insect plaguing the sugar crop. The idea was that the cane toad would eat the insect; in reality, it ate everything but. Its spread has been swift and inexorable; and, being poisonous, it poses an ongoing threat to the indigenous wildlife. If history had been consulted, it would have shown that virtually every introduced species has wreaked havoc on the native ecosystem; the fox, the rabbit and the cat have all proved disastrous immigrants. Even a little more research into the cane toad's previous habits would have had the alarm bells ringing; but no, this was tomorrow's solution today. Ironically, the local wildlife has learned from experience. The native Australian bird the kookaburra, originally threatened by the poisonous gland that the cane toad carries on its back, has learned to flip the creatures over before it rips into the softer, safer underbelly. Fittingly, the bird has had the last laugh.

## 320 Throwing the baby out with the bathwater

Another problem with ignoring history is that we reject, in the name of modernism or progress, a lot of useful knowledge and practical wisdom. Hindsight is a valuable tool that we often acknowledge but rarely use. Preserving the past should go beyond saving old buildings or playing Vivaldi on period instruments—wouldn't the world be a much calmer place if we had the plaintive chants of Hildegard of Bingen as our ringtones rather than the strident aggression of *Mission Impossible* or *Fuck Tha Police*? And wouldn't it be even more pleasant if we had no ringtones at all?

There are aspects of old technologies and social systems that are worth reinvestigating. As society fragments and globalisation marginalises many communities, the co-operative models of the medieval city–states begin to make sense. In the context of the biggest problem facing the planet today—global warming—suddenly ancient power generators like windmills and waterwheels look attractive again. Think of the British railway system, ripped up in the 1950s to make way for the motor car. As motorways become very long parking lots burning fossil fuels like there's no tomorrow, it's a sobering thought that there may indeed be no tomorrow.

## 321 Ignoring the advice of your elders

All right, they can bore you rigid with their endless talk about their health problems but society's elders can teach us a lot. Youth culture has steadily assumed a dominance since the second half of the twentieth century. Before that, the flower of youth was regularly and efficiently plucked by global war, economic recession and disease. But with relative stability and increased spending power, the younger generations began to make themselves felt. The ageing baby-boomer generation, with its reluctance to yield any influence whatsoever, has temporarily put a brake on the phenomenon but even they must eventually die, and the world will soon be spared the awful spectacle of the late-middle-aged shuffling about to The Beach Boys or reunion concerts from The Eagles.

Technology increasingly focuses on the young; the insidious identification of the Tweenies (seven to twelve year olds) as a marketing brand and the inexorable rise of popular culture accelerate the trend. The old find themselves increasingly marginalised and ignored—anyone who witnessed the creation of Iraq after the First World War could have offered some valuable tips on how to avoid the sectarian chaos that followed its invasion; but no, nobody bothered to scour the nursing homes to seek their opinions.

## 322 Forgetting to rotate your tyres

## 323 Neglecting to rustproof

## 324 Losing the arts of mending and repairing

History teaches us continuity, which in turn tells us the value and importance of ongoing maintenance. Rather than throw away something that has broken, why not fix it? Why not look after it in the first place to avoid the need for repair? The disposable society is wasteful, profligate and slowly dooming us all to extinction—darn that sock, patch that elbow, mend the leaky boat before we all sink.

# ROLE MODELS FOR THE INEFFECTIVE

*Number 8*

FREDERICK ALBERT COOK was an explorer and physician; a widely respected Arctic adventurer; friend of Raold Amundsen, surgeon on the 1891 polar expedition led by Robert Peary and hero of the ice-bound Belgian Antarctic expedition of 1897. Yet he died an embittered man, jailed for selling stock in a fraudulent oil exploration company and accused of fabricating his two finest achievements: being the first man to climb Mount McKinley, the highest peak in North America; and being the first man to reach the North Pole, purportedly beating Peary to the prize in 1908. Evidence would suggest that Cook didn't get within cooee of the peak of Mount McKinley and the two Innuit guides he took to the Pole later revealed they had in fact travelled south and perhaps come no closer than 400 miles. It was the scandal of the day, the Great Polar Controversy, and even now intense and vitriolic debate continues between Peary's supporters and those intent on restoring Cook's reputation. Cook's early achievements in polar exploration were noteworthy in their own right; why he should throw his reputation away through these seemingly feeble hoaxes is a mystery.

Born to immigrant parents in New York state in 1865, Cook graduated as a doctor in 1890, although his detractors claim he bought a two-year mail order diploma and was better suited to his original profession of milkman. His first wife died in childbirth. A year later he signed on as surgeon in an Arctic expedition led by his soon-to-be arch-rival Peary, himself a controversial figure who lost eight toes to frostbite during his many trips north of the Arctic Circle. (One other appendage remained intact, however, and Peary managed to father a few illegitimate children to local Innuit women, an exploratory achievement ill-received by his wife when she joined him unexpectedly and had to share an igloo with his pregnant Innuit mistress.) Cook seemed equally unimpressed with Peary and refused to sail with him again—perhaps he feared being next in line when the supply of compliant Innuit women dried up.

Unable to settle back into medical practice—or milk sales—Cook took to the lecture circuit, presenting a semi-vaudevillian show about the polar regions, complete with Eskimos for display. It didn't trouble the box-office records, so he set off as a volunteer with the Belgian Antarctic Expedition in 1897. They seemed ill-equipped for the task and spent most of the time frozen in the ice or drifting in an unscientific fashion around the Bellingshausen Sea. Cook proved himself a valuable team member, keeping up morale and working hard to cut a canal through the ice to free the ship. As surgeon, Cook also kept the expedition free of scurvy by insisting the crew eat raw penguin meat. He earned the respect and admiration of fellow expeditioner Roald Amundsen, who later went on to discover the South Pole, keeping detailed and precise navigational records to avoid the sort of controversy that would soon engulf his penguin-eating companion.

Back from the southern seas, Cook led an expedition (although his critics insist it was a tour group of wealthy backers) to Mount McKinley in Alaska. In 1906, on his second attempt, he claimed to have reached the top. Cook then headed off to the Arctic again, claiming to reach the North Pole with two Innuit companions on 21 April 1908. He recorded the moment in his journal in a style that can only be described as being on the mauve side of purple. Returning south, bad weather forced them to spend almost a year living in a cave until Cook re-emerged to telegraph the news of his discovery a mere five days before Peary announced that he had reached the Pole in April 1909. The *New York Herald* bought Cook's story for $6000 and America was abuzz with his heroic exploits.

Initially, he was believed. After all, he was an experienced and respected explorer with powerful friends in the rarefied world of arctic exploration. But gradually cracks began to appear in his story and they were hastily widened by a disgruntled Peary attempting to discredit the upstart. The McKinley expedition was shown to be false when a photo of Cook proudly waving the flag was proved to have been taken on a smaller peak some nineteen miles from the summit. Cook's sole companion on the final climb, Ed Barrill, later signed an affidavit that they had never reached the top but it seems that he was paid by Peary supporters to do it.

Similarly, holes were shot in Cook's North Pole triumph. Where were the papers and records? Conveniently given to an American hunter in Greenland who buried them after Peary refused to transport them back to America. Lost for all time. The photographic proofs were inconclusive to say the least, Cook's Innuit companions abandoned him and many years later, when his original diary was rediscovered in Europe, few of the dates and events tallied with his public recollections. Peary, and the US scientific establishment, proved intractable enemies—even the US Congress weighed in to denounce Cook as a fraud.

Stung by the criticism, Cook went to Texas to engage in some real fraud. He set up a bogus oil exploration company, the Petrol Producers Association, selling worthless stock in a pyramid scheme to gullible, small-time investors. Federal investigators caught up with him and he was sentenced to fourteen years' jail in 1923. He served six years of his sentence, acting as the night warden of the prison hospital, writing articles and books defending his achievements and lecturing his fellow inmates on polar exploration. Ten years after his parole, broke and humiliated yet pardoned on his deathbed by President Franklin D Roosevelt, he succumbed to complications following a cerebral haemorrhage. Rumours of his death were not greatly exaggerated.

His daughter established the Frederick A Cook Society, a research body devoted to the restoration of his reputation, which remains, how should we say it, a work in progress. Ironically, the claims of his adversary Robert Peary have been equally debunked in recent years and it seems that neither man reached the North Pole at all. Despite his hoaxes, Cook made many significant contributions to arctic exploration—he designed tents, sledges and sleeping bags that revolutionised the craft and his genuine achievements in extreme conditions would have been more than enough to guarantee his place in history. Sadly, he fell victim to hubris and, never satisfied with what he had done, felt the need to invent deeds beyond his reach. There's a lesson in that for all of us.

## 325 Inventing deeds beyond your reach

It's difficult enough to convince people you were the hundredth person to reach the North Pole, let alone the first. Cook desperately wanted fame and its attendant trappings and was prepared to lie to get them. The ineffective often feel a compulsive need to embroider, whether it's falsifying a CV to get a job or pretending you've been rough trekking in Nepal when the nearest you got was a re-fuelling stop in Bangkok en route to a resort in Bali.

## 326 Failing to silence Innuit companions

This is a rare—almost niche—habit of the ineffective. But had Cook beaten it, and arranged for the accidental deaths of his Innuit guides, things might have gone differently. It was inevitable that questions were going to asked, witnesses interrogated. If you perpetrate fraud, make sure your story is bullet proof. Implicate your co-conspirators in some way; discredit them, laugh at their petty, spiteful accusations. When that fails, throw yourself on the mercy of history.

## 327 Not taking sufficient pride in your genuine achievements

Despite the assertions of his most virulent critics, who label him a serial conman and an alcoholic, Cook was a talented and genuine explorer with original ideas—who else would have come up with raw penguin meat to defeat scurvy? Even his namesake, Captain Cook, the greatest mariner of the eighteenth century, could only manage lime juice. But his genuine deeds, too, were not enough for Frederick Cook, a man who was desperate to be number one. Does the second man to reach the North Pole expend any less effort? Do we forget the heroic Scott simply because Amundsen beat him to the South Pole? Are we any less proud of the man who stepped onto the moon just after Armstrong, or what's-his-name who was left in the lunar orbiter? Well, yes, but never forget to be content with what you are capable of honestly achieving.

## 328 Feeling a need to climb tall mountains

Why have we made the mistake of worshipping idiots who feel compelled to climb large pieces of rock? Possibly because they're there, or because they fulfil our primeval need for vicarious danger as today's equivalent of the solo woolly mammoth hunter. But what do extreme adventurers inspire others to do, apart from yet more extreme adventuring? Their skills and talents would be better used on the rescue teams who risk their lives saving these self-centred twits.

# 17
# WHY CAN'T I HAVE THAT?

'You can see the glass as half full or half empty.
But either way, it's still half empty.'
*Anon.*

Use this page to reflect on your disappointments.

Let's take another look at a critical aspect of ineffective behaviour: thinking you can have it all. This conundrum—being told you can have everything and then gradually realising that you can't but still striving for it regardless—is one of the root causes of the modern social malaise. The first questions we should ask are: Why do we want it all? Why aren't we happy with what we have?

The powerful myth of personal self-fulfilment has dogged mankind for millennia. A quest for spiritual completeness is central to many religious philosophies—Buddhism, for example, suggests we all strive to rid ourselves of the duality of our natures so we can reach nirvana and escape the endless cycle of reincarnation. Here's a case in point: wouldn't it be a little easier to not believe in reincarnation in the first place? Why create the problem and then suffer pointlessly striving for a solution? Still, logic has never been a central plank of any religion.

## 329 Being unable to escape the endless cycle of reincarnation

Common to all theologies is an attempt to make sense of an incomprehensible world and to elevate the significance of human life above the mere animalistic, i.e. short, brutal and seemingly pointless. Christianity and Islam promise eternal life for those able to reconcile themselves to the God figure. Equally common to these belief systems is this simple notion that you will ultimately be rewarded only if you do the right thing. Now, what exactly constitutes 'the right thing to do' becomes increasingly codified and complex as the religion, shall we say, matures but the reward remains essentially the same. If things aren't much chop down here, follow this set of rules and you'll be much better off in the next world.

## 330 Believing that the next world will make up for this one

In western societies, things began to change at the end of the medieval period—no, stay with me, this is going somewhere. Religion became less of a staff to lean on for support and more of a stick to be beaten with. The Protestant Reformation brought in a more rigid Christianity—people were now far less adequate in the eyes of the Lord; God became a little more unforgiving. At the same time in the secular world, the move towards a mercantile and then industrial economy further exacerbated this sense of personal inadequacy and isolation. Soon populations began to look for a more material comfort to supplement what little spiritual succour an increasingly unattractive church could provide. The 'here' assumed an importance equal to, if not greater than, the 'hereafter'.

This new-found materialism dovetailed nicely into the manufacturing age—there's no point churning out consumer goods unless someone wants to consume them. People were encouraged to seek fulfilment through material goods and when that initial warm inner glow faltered, to seek some more. Society moved from the co-operative model of the trade guilds and city states to centralised governments and a competitive market; labour and time became commodities. The banking system, freed from the medieval restraint that made usury (the charging of interest) illegal, flourished and the stock market grew. Status, relevance and well-being became increasingly determined by material wealth across the social spectrum, particularly in the burgeoning middle classes.

Enter the concept of continual economic growth. Developed economies are expected to expand at a faster rate than population growth. To fuel this, the existing population has to consume more—bigger cars, flatter televisions, fewer but further away holidays, larger houses. Advertisers make sure we do our patriotic duty and hit the shops as frequently as possible; shopping is now the number one recreational pastime, greater than competitive sport and kinetic sculpture combined.

## 331 Regarding shopping as a leisure activity

## 332 Knowing the price of everything and the value of nothing

## 333 Dreaming of being first in line for the Boxing Day sales

Over-arching these social developments has been the political 'emancipation' of the individual. When the class system was seemingly dismantled, the newly liberated working and middle classes were rashly promised that in the new age of equality everyone could have anything. This is patently not possible. In fact, the more 'liberated' the individual has become in the free market economy, the more tightly the wealth generated has concentrated in the hands of the few. Despite the increased amounts of money and goods produced by the world's economies, we are actually moving back to a pre-eighteenth century model of wealth distribution. But to keep your hands firmly on the aspirational ladder, successive governments of all persuasions have embraced the idea of persuading you that there's room for you at the top, that even you can be in the small demographic band of the very wealthy. If you want it badly enough ...

Of course you do! Who doesn't want a holiday in the Maldives, a media home theatrette or business class travel with your own eyeshade and special socks?

But here's the bad news: not everyone can have it all. That's why there are ten business class seats on the plane and 280 down the back. The entire economy depends on keeping you sitting back there in 57D, gazing longingly up the aisle at 3A.

## 334 Keeping business class special socks (if you ever get them) for home use

## 335 Always asking for a free upgrade

## 336 Believing airline lounges are exclusive and the mahogany panels are real

**337 Feeling a flicker of excitement when you get a CabCharge voucher**

**338 Buying a copy of Richard Branson's biography in-flight**

**339 Asking the cabin crew to sign it**

Is there a more depressing sight than an inter-city flight at the close of the working day? Large, sweating business men in ill-fitting suits, brittle corporate women in ill-suited sweaters, all tightly pressed together tapping away on laptops or brows furrowing in concentration as they plough through *Who Moved My Cheese?* The endless queue for a taxi home, mobile phones out to say goodnight to the kids because a $49 flat cap plan brings us all closer together, stomachs churning with the stress of tomorrow's departmental review that might mean a redundancy package and only one more week for Tiphany at day care?

It's ironic that the more you want to rise above the struggle, the more you have to struggle. And yet we're happy to do it day after day to service an illusory notion of career. Every now and then you're inspired to stay the course by motivational speakers who assure us that despite having lost their legs and one arm in a dreadful Olympic ski trials accident, they've dug deep and made it big in online business. And for a while, with the music pounding as they're wheeled off in their special little trolley, remaining fist punching the air, you believe it. You go back to work, get out a year planner and set some goals. Four months later, you're equally inspired by someone who turned a hairdressing salon into a national chain of stores that's going to break into the world market, and you go back to work to prioritise your goals and highlight those that you connect with spiritually.

## 340 Thinking that walking on hot coals will improve your small business skills

## 341 Believing that you can pay someone else to self-motivate you

## 342 Devising a five-year plan once a year

Why do we lose our new-found inspiration so quickly? Why do all self-help gurus rely on repeat business?

## 343 Finding a successful businessman with no legs inspiring only up to a point

The basic problem is that we're confusing **what we want** with **what we think we want**. Too often, we fall prey to desires that have been manufactured for us. As we strive to fulfil those desires, we mask the central obstacle to achieving them: **we don't really want it enough**. And yet that's difficult to admit, flying as it does in the face of everything that society expects of us: work harder, be more productive and be afraid of losing everything. Not only do we waste much of our lives working towards goals we can never reach, deep down we don't even really want to reach them.

## 344 Forgetting that life is what you miss out on while you're working for a 'better' life

## 345 Not realising that if you try to do less you may achieve more

The aspirationalism of the self-help movement is the modern

equivalent of the promise of eternal salvation. Life is deferred in the eventual hope of something better which never arrives—tomorrow, if it ever gets here, will be the busiest day of the week! Self-fulfilment is like Joseph Heller's Catch-22; you can only be fulfilled when you accept that life is essentially unfulfilling. It's all a journey with a destination that no one really wants to visit.

You have everything when you realise you can never have everything. Profound, no?

# 18
# IS THAT ALL THERE IS?

'Success is relative. It's what we can make of
the mess we have made of things.'
*TS Eliot*

**Nearly finished.**

So what have we learned from our travels through the ineffective person's world? Can any of you honestly say that not one of these habits sounds familiar? Aren't we all ineffective at some point, in some aspects of our lives? Isn't that what being human is all about? Am I going to write a sentence soon that isn't a question?

You see, even experts like me sometimes get it wrong—that last paragraph was stylistically inappropriate and I'll happily be the first to admit it, because now I know that I must accept responsibility (34) without feeling guilt (78) and ocasionally I can't spel (47).

Historically, effectiveness has been measured by very different standards. In the Dark Ages, you were considered effective if you lived to the age of thirty-five. Medieval man would be perfectly happy with a modest smallholding, food in his belly and an annual wassail at the village fete. For the pre-industrial age citizen, an honest craft and the ability to read marked you down as a high-achiever; and even in the nineteenth century, a life lived well in the family home with a job until retirement put you firmly in the effective category. It is only now, with our relentless obsession with 'self-improvement', that we're constantly being told we're no good.

Despite what we are told, not everything that is worth accomplishing is done by targets, deadlines, results and action plans. Not everything of value can be bought. Greatness can be found in the smallest of things—stumbled over, muddled through, won by default or discovered completely by accident. And yet, in a society where every aspect of life can be assigned as an evaluative criterion, we're led to believe that if we become more efficient, we'll become more effective.

## 346 Confusing effectiveness with efficiency

Efficiency is not all it's cracked up to be. The most efficient regime in history was the Nationalist Socialist government of Germany's Third Reich. Everyone knows what a disaster that was, although one wonders how long will that be true for; our collective memory proves fatally brief. The Nazi philosophy was founded on the notion of a super race, a belief in the physical and moral superiority of the Aryan people; anyone else was considered ineffective and was to be eradicated. All aspects of life in the new regime could be quantized, measured and rewarded for their efficiency. For a time, the system thrived, pulling Germany out of depression, building autobahns, running a marvellous Olympic Games and going on to conquer most of Europe.

Thankfully for the sake of humanity, there were others in the world who were even more effective than the Nazis and the Reich that was to last a thousand years was defeated in just under six. Who were these victors? A disparate group of peoples opposed to the dictatorship of fascism who struggled and bumbled their way to victory armed with little but vastly superior numbers and the belief in the dignity of the human being regardless of their individual failings. (Apart from the Soviets under Stalin, of course, but they ultimately came to a sticky end as well, and far be it from me to let historical accuracy get in the way of a good parable.)

## 347 Allowing historical accuracy to get in the way of a good parable

The point—and there is a point—is that we are all, at some time and in some way, ineffective. Those who most strongly wish to advance in life at our expense make it their mission to make us feel more ineffective than we actually are. As someone once said of the strength of capitalism, 'The power of a guinea in your pocket is dependent on its absence in the pocket of another.' By creating desire, they create a feeling of inadequacy that ironically only strengthens the desire. By falsely promising to unleash our full potential, they are only making us worry about how distant that promise seems to be. Their success becomes dependent on our willingness to struggle to emulate it.

So we buy things to make us feel better; we work harder to earn the money to buy more; we study self-help books because they've told us we need to; we seek out the solutions they've created for problems that didn't exist.

Who are these mysterious 'they'? Why does it always seem to be them and us, and why are there so many of us and so few of them? Simple mathematics: no one can be top of the class without the rest of the class. Someone's got to provide the bodies for the successful to clamber over on their way to the top. But if you don't want to end up with a high achiever's footprints all over your back, simply stand aside. Get out of their way. To be a *truly* complete person, you've got to be prepared to read life's report card and accept with contentment whatever place you get.

In a lighter moment, French existentialist funny-man Jean Paul Sartre observed that 'All human actions are equivalent ... and all are on principle doomed to failure.' On the surface, that seems a fairly miserable thing to say; yet, having said it, he felt a lot better. Why worry? Ultimately, I've got nothing to lose so I'll have another Pernod and light up a Gitane. As the economist JK Galbraith remarked when told that economic policy would produce positive results in the long run, 'In the long run we'll all be dead.' Enjoy what you are, and stop wasting time chasing what you're told you could be in the long run.

Life is not a dress rehearsal. No, it's a workshop reading of the first draft of an inadequately written script and the most we can do is make the best of it and hope someone's laid on refreshments.

So, time for one last habit of the highly ineffective:

## 348 Leaving the job half done

# FURTHER READING

The following is a selection of self-improvement literature that you may find useless.

*I'm OK—You're Shit* by Judy Falluni
Allen & Unwin, 2004 (reprinted in error 2005)

An honest account of a daughter's love for the mother she never knew that can be read as a manual for all interpersonal relationships. Basically saying it's okay to feel superior; no one will ever love you unless you do, so why not go for broke? Redefining narcissism as a Self-Esteem Generator™, Falluni favourably compares contemporary role models like Paris Hilton and Donald Trump with the charitable lives of the early mendicants.

*Who Grooved My Cheese?* by Aaron Buckmeister
California Freedom Press, 2001

A treatise on ways to deal with change in the hip-hop, rap and associated sub-cultures, this is essentially written for a niche market but contains some interesting insights into why many in today's music scene regard drive-by shootings as legitimate results-based people-management strategies. Buckmeister is a popular speaker for companies targeting youth demographics, as long as he keeps it short and has plenty of pictures.

*The Path Until Recently Less Travelled* by Gregory Peck
Random House, 2003

A repositioning of the classic self-help tome in the now-crowded alternative spiritualism market. Chapters include Idiot's Guide to Hinduism, Meditation in Less than a Minute for the Time Poor, Buddha Wants Me to be Rich and Why Not Consider Catholicism? If you loved the Lonely Planet series and call yourself a traveller, not a tourist, you'll love this random drift-netting of all the world's cultures that are somehow just better than your own.

*Mein Kampf* by A Hitler
Munich Lifestyle Press, Classic Edition, 2003

Not traditionally associated with self-improvement in polite circles but a powerful motivational tool that can be useful in today's workplace. This Classic Edition comes with racial alternatives that might be better suited to your demographic; ethnic stereotyping and scapegoating have made a big comeback in recent years, so why not get on the oompah-bandwagon? Also included is a handy Pitfalls Guide (losing Battle of Britain, delaying development of atomic bomb, trusting Hess, etc.) that you can consult to avoid making the same mistakes. As an added bonus, you'll receive a forty-part documentary series on the SS, as seen on public broadcasting television.

*POWERRR!!!!* by Antony Baskin-Robbins
Hodder and Stoughton, 1998

Baskin-Robbins's personal presentation of his thesis on self-realisation, sold initially as a series of lecturettes, audio tapes and instructional videos, was a popular motivational road show in the mid-1990s until federal prosecutors shut down the company after a convention at the Miami Hilton ended badly. Several participants, dressed as warriors to connect with their spiritual forebears, were wrapped in banana leaves soaked in paraffin which were then set alight as a test of their inner mental strength. Sadly, chanting their personal fighting mantras failed to prevent third degree burns to 80 per cent of their bodies and their distraught relatives remained unconvinced that this was a hard, but ultimately empowering, life lesson. Baskin-Robbins was jailed on tax-related charges but escaped after motivating his fellow inmates to dig deep. By the time prison authorities discovered the tunnel, the self-styled prince of the Beast Within was in South America delivering keynote speeches at plenary sessions of the Colombian drug cartels.

## *Women Are from Jupiter, Men Are from Lord Howe Island* by Doug and Belinda Sharpe, 2003

This self-published book by Doug and Belinda Sharpe, emotion–behavioural therapists boasting PhDs from the Baskin-Robbins Online University, puts a whole new twist on the Mars/Venus dichotomy so brilliantly recognised by Dr John Gray in his 1996 classic. It follows their earlier volume *Women Are from Andromeda, Men Are from Next Door* and does every bit as much for reconciling the differences between the sexes. Interestingly enough, Belinda was born as Bruce Peterson and the Sharpe marriage is not recognised outside New Zealand. Still, his/her personal journey undoubtedly gives fresh insight into why women can't read maps and men can't patronise.

*Healing with Love* by Rosemary Hutchinson
Wildflower Press, 2001

A moving account of Rosemary's attempts to cure fifteen Bolivian orphans of cancer. Inspired by the Californian peace movement of the late 1960s and filled with a belief in the therapeutic powers of love when combined with a herb found only in New Mexico, Rosemary travelled to Bolivia to meditate, along with 3000 like-minded souls around the world joined by telekinesis, on behalf of the sick children. Unbeknownst to Rosemary, the herb in question caused their weakened immune systems to completely shut down and all died within weeks of her arrival. Still, it was a personally cathartic moment for her, one that led to an appearance on the David Letterman show and a seven figure advance from Miramax. Rosemary sympathetically and poetically tells us how to be on the right side of a lose–win situation.